Exploring the Fife Coastal Path

Hamish Brown is a well-known outdoors writer, lecturer and photographer, the first person to walk all the Scottish Munros in a single trip, an adventure he describes in *Hamish's Mountain Walk* (1978). He has published many other bestselling books, including a family saga *East of West, West of East*, with its climax the Fall of Singapore in 1942. He has lived all his adult life on the Fife coast. He prepared this new edition in his 86th year, walking each section of the route whenever the Covid-19 restrictions of 2020–21 permitted.

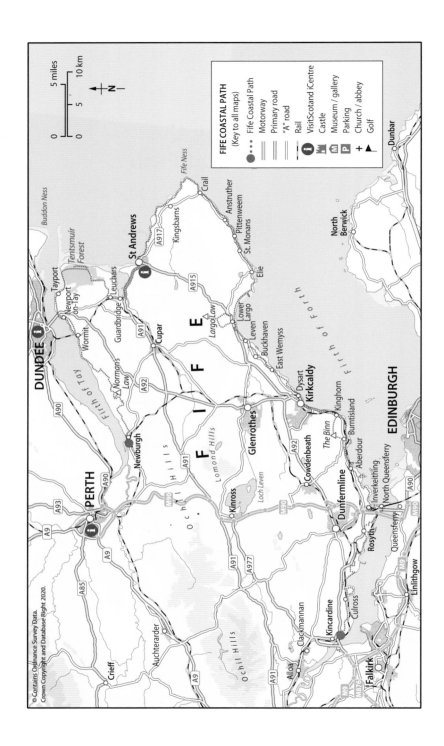

FIFE COASTAL PATH
(Key to all maps)

· · · Fife Coastal Path
Motorway
Primary road
"A" road
Rail
i VisitScotland iCentre
Castle
M Museum / gallery
P Parking
+ Church / abbey
▲ Golf

0 — 5 miles
0 — 5 — 10 km

← N →

DUNDEE

PERTH

A9
A93
A85
A9

Crieff
Auchterarder

A9

Alloa
Clackmannan

A91

Ochil Hills
Ochil Hills

A977
A91

Kinross

Loch Leven

M90

Kincardine
Culross

Dunfermline

Rosyth
Queensferry
North Queensferry
Inverkeithing

M90
A90

FALKIRK
Linlithgow

M9

EDINBURGH

Cowdenbeath
A92

The Binn ▲
Aberdour
Burntisland
Kinghorn

Firth of Forth

Glenrothes

Lomond Hills

F   I   F   E

Newburgh

Ochil Hills

A91

A90

Firth of Tay

Norman's Law ▲

A92

Cupar
A91

Guardbridge
Leuchars
Wormit
Newport-on-Tay
Tayport

Tentsmuir Forest

Buddon Ness

St Andrews
i

A917

Kingsbarns

A915

Fife Ness

Crail
Anstruther
Pittenweem
St. Monans
Elie

Largo Law ▲
Lower Largo
Leven
Buckhaven
East Wemyss

Dysart
Kirkcaldy

North Berwick

Dunbar

EXPLORING THE
FIFE COASTAL PATH

A COMPANION GUIDE

HAMISH BROWN

Hamish Brown
with best wishes

BIRLINN

First published in 2004 by Mercat Press
A second edition published in 2009 by Birlinn Limited
This third edition published in 2021 by
Birlinn Limited
West Newington House
10 Newington Road
Edinburgh
EH9 1QS

www.birlinn.co.uk

Cartography by Helen Stirling

ISBN: 978 1 78027 728 8

British Library Cataloguing-in-Publication Data
A catalogue record for this book is available from the British Library

Designed and typeset in Gill Sans and Palatino
by Tom Johnstone Editorial Services

Printed and bound in Great Britain
by Bell & Bain Ltd, Glasgow

CONTENTS

Maps

INTRODUCTION

Sources of the River Forth lie as far off as the slopes of Ben Lomond and the river falls just eighty feet in 37 miles to where it becomes tidal. Loch Ard is a pretty footnote to the Ben, then, from Aberfoyle onwards, the river twists and turns, circles and loops, through the rich flat farmlands—with names like Faraway, Pendicles of Collymoon, Backside of Garden, Goodie Water, Kersebonny and Barbadoes. At Stirling Geography clashes with History: Stirling Castle, the Wallace Monument, the Stewarts' story, all because here was 'the lowest bridging point' of the Forth. Traffic, trade, armies all had to come this way. Stirling was dubbed 'the bellybutton of Scotland'. And that was how it remained (surprisingly) until 1936 when a bridge was built at Kincardine. This was a swing bridge, as some shipping would head up to Alloa, but it was Kincardine and on to the Forth Bridges triptych that was the commercial, exploitative stretch—what we are setting out to explore at the start of the Fife Coastal Path (FCP).

This runs round the Fife coast, Fife something of a peninsula, lapped by Tay and Forth, with a snout to the North Sea. Kincardine lies just in from the boundary with Scotland's smallest county, Clackmannanshire, and ends just past Newburgh, with Perth and Kinross c. 117 miles (188km) by the FCP. Walking the FCP should take about ten days but I suggest a two-week exploration. I've lived on the Fife coast all my adult life and I'm still finding new interests and surprises.

The FCP is not a demanding mountain trail through remote country demanding necessary disciplines and timetabling, so there is no need to rush it. Make its exploration the primary object, not the ticking off of another listed route. Any official long-distance route has certain restrictions, which pinioning is reflected in guide books. To me it is the exploring that matters, so I can give much more in the way of what to do and see. Guidance for walking the Fife coast could be reduced to six words: 'keep the sea on your right'! Intense guidance is somewhat superfluous. What this book does is indicate the interests (past and present). Take time to explore. Deviate from the signposted FCP. Make discoveries. With so many attractive villages along the way there are also many welcoming cafés and pubs and restaurants (and award-winning chip shops). Make the most of them. To rush is to sin. This guide, by its nature, also appeals to any kind of visitor: the curious traveller above all. You don't have to be a walker—but walking is best.

The FCP originally followed from Forth Bridge to Tay Bridge, which had a pleasing symmetry, entering and leaving Fife by notable features. Since then the FCP has been pushed to cover the whole coast, a proud claim for any county. And what a proliferation of bridges, with the building of the Clackmannanshire Bridge (which touches down in Fife!) and the glorious Queensferry Crossing. At some stage do walk across Forth Road Bridge and Tay Bridge, whether to start/end the FCP or on other occasions. I particularly enjoyed walking into Fife by the Road Bridge and exiting by the Tay Bridge to Dundee to then catch a train to Edinburgh, over the most famous bridge of all. Half of Scotland's population lies within an hour's drive of the Fife coast, and good rail and road systems bring it within easy reach of the rest of the world! The FCP is also part of the grand concept of 'The North Sea Trail'.

It was James VI who described Fife as 'a beggar's mantle fringed with gold', and you won't be allowed to stay ignorant that the fringe was the Fife coast and the gold the export trade from its ports and later the fishing industry. Not much of this prosperity survives. If the salt panning died two centuries ago and industries like shale oil, linen and coal mining have followed, then one gain has been ours, as the squalor of such industries is replaced with rural regeneration and urban renewal. Tourism is big business now, which is one reason the Fife Coastal Path has been developed. Walking a route like this, we actually put our money where our feet are!

The non-walking visitor will equally well find this a useful guide for the towns and sites that dangle like beads on the Fife fringe, but I hope it encourages such to do some walking as well, linking places of interest afoot and so discovering the great benefit to wellbeing that comes from walking. Sir Walter Scott, when work drove him to despair, would go for a good long walk 'to regain his elasticity of mind'.

There is nothing to beat exploring on foot, and the natural linear progression of following a coast also means transport is fairly straightforward, so one can travel to a town, walk, and then, at the day's end, be able to return easily to the start. The whole coast could be explored piecemeal like this but how much more rewarding to win free of the wheeled monsters and for a couple of weeks go footloose and fancy free along the Castles Coast, East Neuk and the 'Silvery Tay'. If you are a walker this is obvious, if you are a nascent walker there's no place better to give 'real' walking a try. You will also be made aware of the voices of nature: skylarks reeling, curlews calling, eiders commenting, seals singing, and the everlasting sounds of wind and water.

For most of the time the route is obvious. 'Continue eastwards' is the most repeated directive, but even this can have odd local quirks. Everyone talks of the east end and the west end of Kirkcaldy High Street, but a glance at the maps shows it runs due north-south! Changes will go on happening too, and any note of these would be welcomed by the author. (Send such addressed to the publishers.)

The FCP does not necessarily indicate what to see and do along the way, especially in the towns, so I don't hesitate to deviate; with this guide we are *exploring* the Fife coast. The panorama from the Binn, the interest of the Kirkcaldy Museum and Art Gallery, the mining tunnels at St Andrews Castle, the charm of the East Neuk villages, Norman's Law— these just have to be explored. There's comfortable tourist accommodation, public transport is adequate. Make use of everything and weave your own cloth of gold.

The two additional stretches of Fife Coastal Path emphasise some practical problems. There is no obvious accommodation available at either Kincardine or Newburgh or along some sections of the FCP. However, this is not as insurmountable a problem as believed. In 2020 I walked the entire FCP, from Kincardine to Newburgh (but breaking it down into much smaller daily distances, as researching/checking everything *en route* for this book) and was, throughout, entirely reliant on public transport. I always found a bed at night using buses or trains. The only place this was not possible was walking the rump of the Ochils and I simply took a taxi from Brunton to Cupar, and back next day. Bus services all along the coast were surprisingly good. Examples: having walked from Kincardine I then spent the rest of the day enjoying Culross, and walking round Preston Island, then caught a bus to Dunfermline; having explored the delights of Cambo I caught a bus back to Crail. There is one soft option, to sign up for one of the tour-operating companies who organise accommodation and provide a baggage transfer service, but they at present stick to Bridges to Bridges. Another trick on the busier, touristy parts, to stay on in a B&B for successive nights and using bus or taxi to return to the known comforts. We can only hope as more people tackle the whole FCP (likewise the Fife Pilgrim Way) the local facilities will appear to meet the need; after all, the first and last sections add considerable character and interest to the FCP. Dealing with these kinds of problems is both part of the fun and frustration of any worthwhile challenge. Note too, many sites and services close from October to Easter while, post the Coronavirus period, some listed facilities may not have survived. Check whatever you can; ahead. If phoning a B&B, obtain directions of how to find it. Lastly, if the British Open Golf Championship is being played at St Andrews, every bed in the East Neuk will be taken and the St Cuthbert's Way would be a better option. On several occasions the route edges golf courses and it is only courteous not to disturb play. Stand still and watch (which sometimes causes *more* nervousness!) and keep dogs in control (players don't really want golf balls 'fetched') but, quite seriously, watch out for flying golf balls. (The Golf Museum in St Andrews has a stuffed skylark in a glass case, along with the ball that struck it dead in flight.)

The importance of Fife historically is seen in most of the coastal towns being Royal Burghs: Inverkeithing, Kinghorn and Crail as early as the twelfth century, Burntisland, Dysart, Pittenweem and Anstruther in the sixteenth century, Kirkcaldy and St Andrews in the next century, though they are now the biggest towns on the coast. Newburgh had its charter confirmed by Charles I. One result of this background is the surviving architectural and historical richness: castles, churches, tolbooths, harbours, doocots, milestones and red-roofed 'little houses'. Every town seemed to have a harbour, ferries abounded and Fife was criss-crossed with routes taking pilgrims to St Andrews, courtiers to the one-time capital of Dunfermline or Falkland (the Stewarts' Balmoral) or merchants to the mines of Culross and the wheatlands of Cupar, or royal corpses to Inchcolm, which followed Iona as the burial place of kings. The Forth and Tay also gave Fife a natural unity if not insularity. Fife was not easily invaded, with the 'lowest bridging points' being Stirling or Perth. Even the Romans hardly touched Fife. (But you can read later why I live next to Cromwell Road.)

There are still some sorry sights/sites along the way, more now from personal vandalism than the industrial past (the Fife authorities have had international recognition for their 'green' efforts) and one of the best defences against such misuse is the presence of people. People are the best deterrent to vandalism and I feel, too, as things improve, there is less inclination to damage. Late, late, too, we are beginning to realise the sea is not a sewer or rubbish dump, but it will take generations yet to undo the damage from dumping Frances or Randolph colliery redd (spoil) into the Forth. The estuary still sees something like 6500 ship movements a year (numbers fall as tonnage rises). The walk gives quite a mix of rural peace and town bustle.

A few more practical points. Heights on the map are given in metres and I see no sense in converting these any longer. Distances are given in miles. As grid squares are 1km across it is hardly difficult to calculate kilometres (8km = 5 miles is a useful guide), and a yard and a metre are close enough for smaller measurements. There are plenty of official signposts at stations and in the towns indicating the FCP and also along its length, but beware, some may be missing and, of course, we frequently take our own way rather than always following the FCP. But it is our route for much of the way, and as such doesn't need mentioned at every signpost or waymark. Carry and use the maps. You will want to know what you are looking at on those big views. And don't confuse cycleway signs and FCP ones; they can differ. I usually mention the mileage ahead. The total is about 117 miles.

The word *road* always implies a tarred surface and public use, *track* will be unsurfaced but motorable and may or may not be private for vehicles while quite walkable, *path* means a route only practical on foot. Most of what is described will be right-of-way or a created route, but there may be places which are technically private. If behaviour is sensible there should be no problems. 'Walk softly, take nothing but photographs, leave nothing but memories.' Remember too, we share the land with other users. (I've heard of walkers complaining because there were sheep on the path!) Savour the sea too. Paddle. Swim. Feel the flukies under your toes or find butterfish below the seaweeds. Walk the vast sands. Watch the abundant bird life. Enjoy pub chat and a haggis supper, B&B and gourmet dining. Make it a fun walk.

Many of the towns are popular summer resorts and there are advantages in going in spring or autumn. Sharp winter days can be good but some attractions will not be open. July and August may still give richer rewards than the 3M flaws of the Highlands: mobs, midges and monsoon. Rainfall on the coast is fairly slight but it can be cold, especially if an east wind is coming from Russia without much love. In the height of summer some woodland spots can suffer from a plague of flies. No logic. No warning. Nothing to do except walk on.

The tides will make or mar some sections, so become aware of their movement from the start. Tide tables, set to Leith, are available but it is largely a matter of using one's eyes. Burntisland tides, where I live, are the same as Leith, while Inverkeithing is Leith +9 minutes, Methil −9, Elie −17 and Fife Ness −21. If warnings are needed they will be given in the text, and there are few if any problems an hour or two either side of high tide, so don't over-react to this problem. (There are no such problems on the River Tay.)

Wild camping is difficult (scarce drinking water) but more camping facilities are appearing.

The route is usually given as a 9–10-day walk, but most people would want to take longer if looking at all the interests along the way, and at least a day would be needed to explore St Andrews. With reasonable transport, moving about the eastern parts is easy, so a wide range of accommodation opens up. One could use a B&B for several days in a row even. It is perhaps safest to book accommodation ahead day by day. It is a great relief to know the bed for the night is secure.

While every care has been taken to describe the route accurately, neither author nor publisher accepts responsibility regarding information, or its interpretation by readers. Signposts vanish (or are turned round!), brambles grow, paths vanish under new roads or housing schemes. Before many years I'm sure there will be plenty alterations. As many are improvements, I hope so. While welcoming information on changes, entering into correspondence on such matters is not possible. There should always be an expectation of the unexpected on any walk. We explore and walk the Fife coast for fun. To create memories. Enjoy!

Hamish Brown
Burntisland 2021.

PRACTICAL INFORMATION

Sites and facilities may be seasonable and many have complicated opening hours, or certain days closed and are apt to change, so checking ahead is advisable; otherwise one takes 'pot luck'. Venues are listed under their town (e.g. for *Byre Theatre* see under St Andrews). Be aware that post-coronavirus there may be changes or closures not recorded here.

Tourist Information

St Andrews Tourist Information Centre is the only such now in Fife but you may find some information available at major venues such as the Kirkcaldy Galleries, the Fisheries Museum, Crail Heritage Centre. Large Information Centres also exist in Dundee and Edinburgh.

St Andrews Tourist Information Centre, 70 Market Street, KY16 9NU. Tel: 01334-472021.

Dundee Tourist Information Centre, 16 City Square, DD1 3BG. Tel: 01382-527527.

Edinburgh Tourist Information Centre, 3 Princes Street, EH2 20P. Tel: 0131-473-3800.

Transport

Traveline Scotland: Tel: 0871-2002233, www.travelinescotland. com.

Rail enquiries: www.nationalrail.co.uk

Bus services: the main bus service providers are Stagecoach East Scotland (01383-660880, www.stagecoachbus.com) and Moffat & Williamson (01382-541159, www.moffat-williamson.co.uk).

Fife Council: www.fifedirect.org.uk. www.travelfife.com is a new comprehensive travel guide to the area.

Taxis: often a forgotten option and readily available in the coast towns and villages.

If still published there are three complete guides covering Fife bus services, however all bus station offices are being closed. Nicolson's *Fife Street Atlas* (2020) is of interest.

Tide Times

Coastguard, Tel: 01224-592354, www.tides4fishing.com.

Countryside Ranger Services

Ranger services can be found at Craigtoun Country Park (01334-473666), Lochore Meadows (01592-414300) and in the Lomond Hills Regional Park (01592-583240).

Sites and Services

Aberdour Castle. Tel: 01383-860519. Seasonal (Historic Scotland).

Adam Smith Centre (see Kirkcaldy)

Anstruther, Scottish Fisheries Museum. Tel: 01333-310628, www. scottishfisheriesmuseum.org.

Balmerino Abbey. Open all year (NTS).

British Golf Museum (see St Andrews).

Buckhaven Museum, 63 College Street (in local library). Tel: 01592-583202.

Burntisland Beacon Leisure Centre. On seafront. Tel: 01592-583383.

Burntisland Church. Tel: 01592-872139 to arrange opening.

Burntisland Edwardian Fair Museum, Library Building, 102 High Street. Tel: 01592-583203. Open library hours.

Burntisland Heritage Trust, 4 Kirkgate. Tel: 01592 872121. Seasonal exhibitions.

Burntisland Museum of Communications, 131 High Street. Tel: 0842-8163952, www.mocft.co.uk.

Byre Theatre (see St Andrews)

Cambo Gardens, Kingsbarns. Tel: 01333-450054. Open all year.

Crail Museum and Heritage Centre, Marketgate. Tel: 01333-450869, www.crailmuseum.org.uk.

Crail Pottery. Tel: 01333-451212.

Crawford Art Centre (see St Andrews)

Culross, Royal Burgh of. Tel: 01383-880359, www.nts.org.uk. Open all year (NTS).

Deep Sea World (see North Queensferry)

Dysart, Harbourmaster's House. Tel: 01592-656080. Open daily. Bistro, Tel: 01592-654862.

East Sands Leisure Complex (see St Andrews)

Eden Estuary Centre. For entry, phone FC and CT, Tel: 01592-656080 or Ranger, Tel: 07985-707593.

Falkland Palace. Open Easter-October (NTS).

Fife Coast and Countryside Trust. Authority for the Fife Coastal Path, based in the Harbourmaster's House, Dysart. Tel: 01592-656080, www.fifecoastalpath.co.uk.

Guardbridge Brewery and Distillery, Tel: 01333-158337

Historic Scotland (Historic Environment Scotland). Tel: 0131-6688999.

Inchcolm Abbey. Tel: 01383-823332. Open: Easter—September (Historic Scotland). Ferry from Hawes Pier, Queensferry (*Maid of the Forth*) Tel: 0131-3315000.

Kirkcaldy, Adam Smith Theatre. Tel: 01592-583306. Open all year. Café.

Kirkcaldy Galleries (Museum and Art Gallery). Tel: 01592-538206. Open all year as Library hours (same building). Café.

Kirkcaldy Leisure Centre, Esplanade. Tel: 01592-583306. Open all year.

Levenmouth Pool and Sports Centre (Leisure Centre). Tel: 01333-659325. Open all year.

Lindores Abbey Distillery. Tel: 01337-842547. Open all year.

May Island. Sailings for/from Anstruther, *May Princess*. Tel: 07597-585200, www.anstrutherpleasurecruises.co.uk. *Osprey and Osprey II* (RIBS). Tel: 07437-631671, www.isleof-mayboattrips.co.uk.

Methil Heritage Centre. 272 High Street. Tel: 01334-659339. Open: Tues-Thur.

Newburgh Laing Museum, 120 High Street. Tel: 01334659380 (limited opening).

North Queensferry, Deep Sea World. Tel: 01383-411880. Open all year.

North Queensferry, Forth Sea Safaris. Tel: 07752-156733, www.forthseasafaris.co.uk.

Pittenweem, St Fillan's Cave. Open all year. Notice indicates where to obtain key.

Ravenscraig Castle. Open all year. No custodian; parts locked (Historic Scotland).

Silverburn Park. Open all year, dawn to dusk. Tel: 01333-278775. Café, restaurant, pods, camping.

St Andrews Aquarium. Tel: 01334-474786.

St Andrews, Botanic Gardens, Canongate. Tel: 01334-476452. Open all year. (Tropical butterfly house.)

St Andrews, British Golf Museum. Tel: 01334-460046, www. britishgolfmuseum.co.uk. Open all year.

St Andrews, Byre Theatre, 36 South Street. Tel: 01334-475000.

St Andrews Castle and Visitor Centre. Tel: 01334-477196. Open all year (Historic Scotland).

St Andrews Cathedral and Museum. Tel: 01334-472563. Open all year (Historic Scotland). At either Castle or Cathedral, a ticket can be bought to cover both sites.

St Andrews East Sands Leisure Centre. Tel: 01334-659473. Open all year.

St Andrews Museum, Kinburn Park. Tel: 01334-659380. Open all year. Café.

St Andrews Preservation Trust Museum and Garden, 12 North Street. Tel: 01334-477629. Seasonal.

St Andrews, Wardlaw Museum, aka MUSA (Museum of the University of St Andrews). 7a The Scores. Tel: 01334-461660.

St Monans Windmill. Interior open summer only.

Maps

OS 1:50,000 Landranger sheets 59, 65 and 66, and 1:25,000 Explorer sheets 367, 370 and 371 cover the route. The relevant map numbers are given at the start of each chapter.

Glossary

Some names encountered or on the map may puzzle.

burn: stream

causeys: squared-off cobbles (setts), streets of such

close: passage access to flats/narrow lane

crowstep gables: squared stones like steps on the gable, often where there are pantiles which were laid from a plank resting on the steps.

den: dell/lowland glen

doocot: dovecote

dyke: a wall (or geological feature looking like such)

gait: street (e.g. Seagait)

glebe: parish minister's land

law: hill

links: seaside grassy area/common/golf course

manse: home of parish minister

marriage lintel: husband and wife's initials, usually over door, marking the completion of construction rather than the marriage date

ness: headland/point

pend: passage through a building/or under railway

port: ancient town gateway, sometimes porte

redd: mining waste material

tollbooth: medieval town offices (often incorporating a prison cell)

well: in Scotland covers any water source—spring, fountain, even a tap

wynd: lane

yett: door(way)

Pronunciation

This is shown when introducing places which are apt to cause confusion; both Scots and English having the habit of making the written and vocal quite different in place names. (There are local pronunciations as well: Buck-hyne for Buckhaven, Ainster for Anstruther, Balmernie for Balmerino etc., but these won't concern visitors.) If the English think it is only Scotland that gives such problems then think again, from as simple names as Derby and Keswick.

Aberdour: aber-dower

Burntisland: burnt-island

Culross: coo-rus

Elie: ee-lee

Kincardine: kin-car-din

Kirkcaldy: kir-coddy

Longannet: long-annat

Wormit: Wer-mit

Abbreviations

NTS: National Trust for Scotland

SWT: Scottish Wildlife Trust

HS: Historic Scotland (Historic Environment Scotland)
SSSI: Site of Special Scientific Interest
SPA: Special Protection Area

Bookshops

Sites visited will often carry interesting local booklets. On the Fife coast Waterstones have shops at 171 High Street, *Kirkcaldy*, Tel: 01592-263755 and at 101-103 Market Street, *St Andrews*, Tel: 01334-477893.

St Andrews New books, Topping and Company, 7 Greyfriars Gardens, Tel: 01334-595111 and also a good antiquarian/second-hand shop, Bouquiniste, 31 Market Street, Tel: 01334-476724; while Barnardo's (Bell Street) and Oxfam (South Street) have bookshops (second-hand).

Burntisland has a large second-hand bookshop, Hanselled Books, Kirkgate, Tel: 01592 873323.

It may be worth carrying a flower and/or bird book with you.

Further Reading

Here a few books, for reference, or following up interests, which I have enjoyed.

Allan, J., *The Isle of May* (Tervor Ltd, 2000). The best general guide.

Baird, B., *Shipwrecks of the Forth and Tay* (Whittles, 2008).

Bardwell, S. and Megarry, J., *Fife Coastal Path* (Rucksack Readers, 2018). Best current straight guide book in waterproof, ringback form. Has updates.

Bathurst, B., *The Lighthouse Stevensons* (Harper, 1999).

Bradley, I., *The Fife Pilgrim Way* (Birlinn, 2019). Comprehensive historical/architectural guide.

Brockie, K., *One Man's Island* (Harper and Row, 1984). May Island.

Brockie, K., *Return to One Man's Island* (Birlinn, 2012). A bird artist's evocative work.

Brodie, I., *Steamers of the Forth* (David and Charles, 1976).

Brown, H. M., *A Scottish Gravestones Miscellany* (Birlinn, 2008). Topical/historical study.

Bruce, W. S., *The Railways of Fife* (Melven Press, 1980).

Corbett, G. B. (ed.), *The Nature of Fife* (Scottish Cultural Press, 1988). Wildlife and ecology.

Christie, G., *Harbours of the Forth* (Johnson, 1955).

Fawcett, R. and McRoberts, D., *Inchcolm Abbey and Island* (HMSO, 1990).

Frazer, D., *Historic Fife* (Melven Press, 1982). Good background; illustrated.

Frazer, D., *Illustrious Fife* (Akros, 1998). Literary, historical, topographical.

Gifford, J., *Fife* (Yale University Press, 2003). Pevsner-style: comprehensive on architecture.

Glen, D. and Hubbard, T., *Fringe of Gold: The Fife Anthology* (Birlinn, 2008).

Hendrie, W. F., *The Firth of Forth* (John Donald, 1998).

Kinninmouth, S., *Fife Folk Tales* (History Press, 2017).

Low, L., *St Andrews' Untold Stories* (Savage, 2015). (Also *Largo's Untold Stories*, 2013 and *The Battle of St Monans*, 2017.) Interesting shorter works.

Macdonald, S., *The Witches of Fife* (John Donald, 2002).

Macintyre, L. and Adamson, P., *Portrait of the East Neuk* (Alvie Press, 1999).

Mackay, S., *The Forth Bridge: A Picture History* (Mowbray House, 1990).

McMullan, S., *Hidden St Andrews* (Black and White, 2014). Pictures and text on sites.

Moffat, A. and Brown, G., *Fife* (Deerpath Press, 2019). History.

Neeley, K. A., *Mary Somerville* (Cambridge University Press, 2001).

Peterkin, G. A. G., *Scottish Dovecotes* (Culross, 1980).

Pride, G. L., *The Kingdom of Fife: An Illustrated Architectural Guide* (RIAS, 1990. Excellent.

Prebble, J., *The High Girders* (Secker, 1956). The Tay Bridge story.

Reid, N. H., *Ever to Excell: An Illustrated History of the University of St Andrews* (Dundee University Press, 2011).

Rush, C., *A Twelvemonth and a Day* (Aberdeen University Press, 1985). A striking novel on a Fife fishing community, made into a film, *Venus Peter*.

Scott-Bruce, W., *The Railways of Fife* (Melven Press, 1980).

Stephen, W., *The Story of Inverkeithing and Rosyth* (Moray Press, 1938).

Stevenson, S., *Anstruther* (John Donald, 1989).

The Statistical Accounts of Scotland were a series of parish surveys carried out at roughly century intervals and give information on everything at the time. *The First* appeared 1791-1799, a reprint of Fife in 1978; *The New Statistical Account of Scotland*, Vol. 9, Fife, 1845; *The Third Statistical Account of Scotland: County of Fife*, ed. Smith, A., 1952.

Thomas, D., *Cochrane, Britannia's Sea Wolf* (Andre Deutsch, 1978).

Wilkie, J., *Bygone Fife: from Culross to St Andrews* (Blackwood, 1931).

COAST AND COUNTRY CODE

Before leaving home:

- Acquire adequate waterproofs, comfortable boots and emergency items.
- If going alone, organise some system of phoning home or to someone acting as base. If you break a leg by the Kenly Water it is nice to know someone will be worried sooner rather than later.
- Learn something of elementary first-aid and prepare a small field kit. (Blisters the commonest complaint.) Plan within your capabilities. Tired people are far more accident-prone.

Read up about the areas being visited. The curious traveller is usually the happiest traveller. Buy all the maps you need and read through this book *with* the maps.

During the walk:

- Close all gates. There is nothing calculated to annoy farmers more than having to round up strayed livestock. Don't go over walls or through fences or hedges.
- Leave livestock, crops and machinery alone.
- Guard against all risk of fires.
- Dump your litter in bins, not on the shore or in the countryside. You'll see some bad sights, so don't add to them. Polythene bags can mean disaster to a grazing cow, broken glass is wicked for both man and beast, and drink cans are an insufferable eyesore. (Why not pick up some litter as you go?)
- Leave wildlife alone. Collecting eggs or flowers is illegal. 'Lost' creatures are rare; parents will soon find their young unless some unhelpful person has carried them off.
- Walk quietly in the countryside. Nature goes unobtrusively and you'll see far more if you are not clad in garish colours and walking with intrusive music in your ear.
- While most of this trip is on rights-of-way or other established walking routes, it is still running through a farmed and used landscape, so treat it with respect. Local people's livelihood depends on this countryside. There is no wilderness.

- Dogs are a mixed blessing. In sheep/farming country they need strict control so neither dog nor owner can relax much. In the lambing season (February-May) dogs are particularly unwelcome.
- Be extra careful when walking on roads, however quiet these appear. Maniac drivers and cyclists are no respecters of pedestrians.
- Keep an eye on incoming tides. Do not pick up unusual or mystery objects from the beach. Report them to the police.
- Swimming may be dangerous and is best kept for recognised beaches.
- Make local contacts. Rural people are still sociable and a 'crack' will often be welcomed. Those met in bars, cafés or overnight stops are often a fund of information. They may even find *us* interesting.

It is rewarding to keep a record of some kind, one's own notes and photographs, perhaps with added postcards, drawings, anything that appeals. In later years a record like this becomes a treasured souvenir.

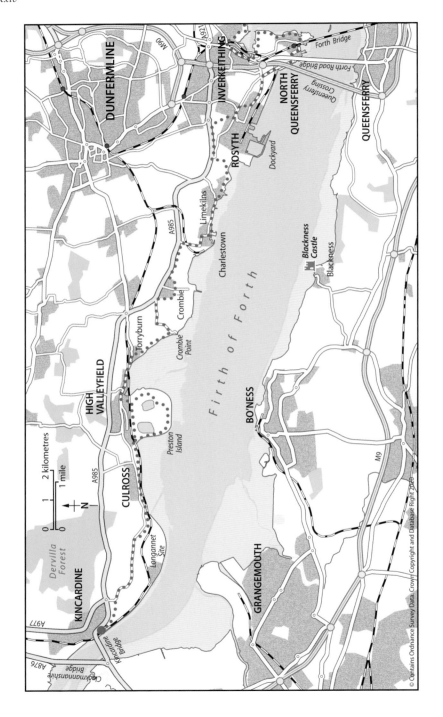

Forth Bridge

Forth Road Bridge

Queensferry
Crossing

INVERKEITHING

DUNFERMLINE

NORTH
QUEENSFERRY

ROSYTH

QUEENSFERRY

Dockyard

A985

Limekilns

Charlestown

Blackness
Castle

Blackness

Crombie

Torryburn

Crombie
Point

Firth of Forth

HIGH
VALLEYFIELD

BO'NESS

Preston
Island

CULROSS

M9

Dervilla
Forest

A985

Longannet
Site

GRANGEMOUTH

KINCARDINE

Kincardine
Bridge

Clackmannanshire
Bridge A876

A977

N

2 kilometres

1 mile

0   1   2

0   1

© Contains Ordnance Survey Data, Crown Copyright and Database Right 2020

I
The Upper Forth Reaches: Kincardine Bridge to Forth Bridges

O.S. 65/367

Back in the nineteenth century Kincardine and Culross were a 'detached' part of Perthshire. (Boundary changes are not new.) Kincardine today seems a sleepy, unpretentious sort of place and it is hard to envisage that, in the eighteenth and nineteenth century its shipbuilding activity was second only to Leith on the Forth. (In 1812, 15 vessels were recorded 'on the stocks'.) There were fifteen salt pans in 1780. Steamers called on a Granton-Stirling service and there was a ferry across the half mile of river. One odd statistic: in 1881 the population was 1985, of whom 1141 were female. The only notable born in Kincardine was the scientist Sir James Dewar (1842-1923) to whom walkers are indebted: he invented the thermos flask.

The official Fife Coastal Path (FCP begins at Kincardine; 'at' rather than 'in' for it is slap up beside the dual carriageway near the bridge, with traffic speeding past or tailing back when busy. There are pedestrian lights to reach it, however I'd suggest a far pleasanter start—from the 1675 market cross in the High Street. That is where buses stop and parking is possible. The name is pronounced Kin-car-din (I was once asked the way to Kinker-deane).

Before setting off there is one place to discover: a kirkyard with one of the country's best displays of eighteenth-century gravestones, notably those showing trade symbols. Head along the High Street and cross the A977 to Kirk Road. The church lies at the far end but the kirkyard gate is locked. Pick up the key from the café on the left starting up Kirk Street. Because stones have been re-erected where necessary and all are cleaned the carvings are beautifully clear. With the town's maritime history many show ships (perhaps owned by the person interred; there were 50 ship owners in Kincardine in 1823), or ships being built (one has a wright and apprentice shown at work), navigation instruments, an

Shipwrights at work on a Tulliallan gravestone.

anchor (the 'wrong way' up indicates 'anchored in heaven'), the sock and coulter of farmers, the crown and hammer of hammermen (all who worked in metal), the tools of a miner and even a tree-feller. Because much trade was with the Baltic, when winter froze the ports, many took up a separate winter trade, such as mariner and weaver, or farmer, or mason, and this duality will be shown on a stone's having two symbols.

For the Fife Coastal Path set off trom the High Street sea-wards, cross a street and continue down Keith Street. (Looking left at the crossing you'll see the attractive clock tower.) This is a street of handsome older houses and when Keith Street swings right one 'auld hoose' (old house) has a marriage lintel for JJ and KS dated 1734. Steps go up to the end of the Kincar-dine on Forth Bridge (its full name) and a quick visit to stand on the fine bridge gives a pleasing view upriver. Near is the Clackmannanshire Bridge, which actually touches down in Fife. The new bridge was designed by W.A. Fairhurst & Co. (who built the Tay Bridge) and is the world's second longest 'incrementally launched' bridge—pillars being sunk and the bridge then pushed outwards. There are 26 spans.

The Ochils lie off right and on our last day of the FCP we will walk their lower, eastern end. The Wallace Monument shows well and also Ben Ledi and Ben Lomond, if lucky.

Return to Keith Street but almost at once turn left to walk under the bridge (cycleway 76 sign). That's it, now you come to the official FCP, the official start just up left, a rather fine arch in the FCP colours set on artistic pillars. A good view of the bridge too. Culross lies four miles ahead.

The Kincardine Bridge was the first to span the Forth from Fife, opening in 1936, and becoming the new 'lowest bridging point'. Kincardine Bridge was all too well known to people waiting for the Queensferry ferry. Commuters to Edinburgh knew the exact spot in the queue when it would be quicker to go round by Kincardine. Kincardine Bridge's engineer was Sir Alexander Gibb, who was given the remit of the bridge still allowing ships to pass upriver, so the bridge's central section pivots. I was lucky enough to see it in action before it closed in 1988.

Sheltering from rain below the bridge with only a map for companion I was thinking of the East Neuk's reputation for unusual place names, so had a look at the map of this end of Fife to see what I could find. Balbougie, Gallowridge,

Kincardine Bridge.

Boats at Kincardine, Longannet beyond.

Blinkeerie, Burrowine, Pit-conochie, Bouprie Banks, Stand Alane, Ashes . . . Not so bad, and so thoroughly Lowland Scottish.

There's some proliferation of FCP and Cycle Routes signs and all the way to Culross paths, wide or narrow, are shared. You are warned; cyclists seldom have the manners to announce their arrival at your side. It must be a sort of ego thing: sissy to have a bell, embarrassing to shout. We have a roar of traffic on our left to begin with and march towards the chimney of Longannet ahead. We are on tarmac throughout this section, good for cyclists but hard on the feet of walkers. We pass a timberyard making stobs (posts) of all sizes. (At Burntisland they make pallets.) At the entrance to the now ex-power station we cross over to a cycle/walkway on the seaward side of the Culross road. Fortunately the traffic is now more minutes per car than cars per minute and we wend through pretty enough countryside. At one place there's an open space (two lines of pylons) which gives us the only good near view of Longannet (pronounced Long-annat, nothing to do with a certain seabird).

Completely gone is any sign of the last deep coal mine in Scotland, which fed this last coal-burning giant through underground tunnels. When Longannet was up and running (1973) it was the largest such construction in Europe. Closure came in 2016 and it was planned to be decommissioned by 2020. Will it all be demolished? Many would miss a lifelong landmark in the stocky 183-metre chimney. The site is being redeveloped by the giant firm Talgo and they will be making railway stock. (I once travelled on the Talgo Express from Madrid to the Spanish border.)

Eventually our wendy way turns down to the *coast* where there is a notice for Torry Bay Nature Reserve; there mainly for the benefit of winter waders. The rusty railway runs between us and the shore for the next long straight ('which feels longer'), there are some reedbeds on the left and up in the woods the site of Donimarle Castle where Lady Macduff and her children were murdered. The Royal Burgh (and Conservation Area) of Culross is reached at a carpark. The pronunciation is Coo-rus.

At the far end of the carpark there is a huge anchor and an ice house (centuries ago filled with ice to act as a sort of fridge). Information boards point out the Moat Pit lying out to sea: a mere seaweedy bump now but once a masonry tower, an exit from coal workings below, an extraordinary object for the seventeenth century. The pit was drained by a conveyor of buckets operated by literal horse power. Attached wooden quays would see ships loaded with coal. A storm in 1625 destroyed the works, flooding the mine. James VI is supposed to have come through from the shore underground/undersea, and on popping out to find himself apparently marooned yelling, 'Treason! Treason!' (He did reign for 58 years, a record for the unchancy Stuarts.)

On a bit, you can cross to the restored pier or use a right of way squeezed between railway and sea to continue (it is part of the West Fife Woodlands Way [*sic*]) but one cannot bypass Culross; I'll come back to this afterwards. When the left opens up as the Green (play area, left), you are looking at the unique gem that is old Culross. I once overheard

Culross: Tanhouse Brae.

Culross Palace.

someone, asked about shops, commenting 'There's none.
It's all Legoland.' Bang on.

Crossing over, there's an obvious bust, in naval uniform,
of Thomas Cochrane, who became 10th Earl of Dundonald.
To our then French enemies he was the *loup de mer* (sea wolf)
during a career as fabulous as Nelson's. He never received the
recognition or rewards from the Admiralty he deserved and
later hired himself to both Chile and Brazil where his naval
prowess led directly to them gaining independence. (They
cheated on him too.) He was an MP and an inventor with
ideas far ahead of his time. There's a eulogy on the ground in
front of the monument. Cochrane well exemplified the adage
'Truth can be stranger than fiction' and Patrick O'Brian in
his Jack Aubrey series of naval stories uses whole chunks of
recognisable Cochrane epics—on which the film *Master and
Commander* was based. Culross also appeared as a location in
Outlander: the village Cranesmuir.

Behind and partly hidden by January House is the great
showpiece of Culross Palace in its mustard-yellow wash, 'a
confusing complex of adjacent buildings'. Strictly speaking

it was a fine Laird's house, built in 1597 to 1611 by George, later Sir George Bruce. This change in status can be seen in an inscription and date 1597 with GB, but in 1611 it was SGB (Sir George Bruce). He was an entrepreneur who made a fortune from coal and spent on buildings to reflect his status, a lot of it three storeys high and the windows half glazed, half shuttered, a novelty at the time.

The greatest features inside are the painted ceilings (beams and walls too), of the Great Hall and the study/strong room. You can see period furniture, ceramics and pewter—and a rather battered example of a Culross girdle (iron baking plate for making scones, oatcakes etc). The metal workers, hammermen, had a monopoly on making these, a craft important enough that they had their own gallery in the church. Cheaper girdles turned out by the Carron Iron Works killed that business. Don't overlook the Palace Garden, a practical seventeenth-century design for producing fruit and vegetables. If you encounter a hen it is a Scots Dumpy, from which later breeds came. Bessie's Tearoom is also a popular spot in the Palace. (There's also the Biscuit Café at the Culross Pottery.)

Two fine white houses are central with the Town House next again. It was built in 1626 and rebuilt in 1783. In front is a post set in stone marking the 1625 Tron. A tronmaster was responsible for the weighing of cargoes, here mostly coal. Ships at one time loaded at a quay just where the bus shelter is today. Walk along for the real 'tour', heading up the Back Causeway

Culross.

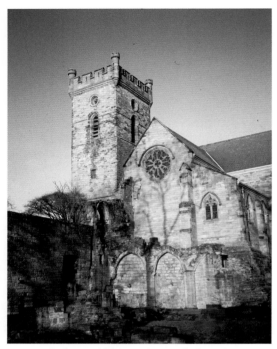

Culross Abbey ruins and church.

(signed for Study, Abbey). Walking up the commanding feature is Bishop Leighton's Study with an attractive tower and
split windows as at the Palace. Before it, left, is Hagg's Wynd.
Names can fascinate. The Market Cross (1588) has an ornate
top with a heraldic unicorn finial. Continuing uphill (Tanhouse
Brae) the orangey house, left, is dated 1664. It and a score of
others bear small National Trust for Scotland markers, indicating the Trust's work over decades to save decaying Culross,
from poorest house to Palace, and see them come to life again.
Most of the houses have entrance steps over a gutter. There are
odd inscriptions too. Look at the names: Old Schoolmaster's
House, Snuff Cottage, Coachman's Cottage. Left, on Erskine
Brae, have a look at the Lockit Well. We're now on Kirk Street
(Cat's Close on the right) which ends at the Abbey ruins. Near
the entrance gate is a marker on the ground marking the start
of the 55-mile Fife Pilgrim Way to St Andrews.

Tradition has St Serf founding a religious community here
in the sixth century and legend adds Kentigern (St Mungo),
supposedly born of a cast ashore refugee mother. The Abbey

The Bruce Mausoleum.

was founded in 1217 by Earl Malcolm of Fife and survived until the Reformation when the east choir was made into the Parish Church (1633). The rest soon fell into decay. The Manse was built from the stone of the west choir. Unlike anything else in Scotland is the tomb of Sir George Bruce (d. 1625). He and his wife pose, lifesize, in white alabaster, while before them kneel their eight adult children! Another Bruce has his heart set in a wall, one Edward, who fought a duel with the Earl of Dorset in 1614 at Bergen op Zoom in the Netherlands and was killed. Fifers seem to have been a quarrelsome people. Other places along the FCP where duels were fought were Aberdour, Kirkcaldy and Newburgh.

The kirkyard is also of interest. Most obvious is a black marble stone to Colour-sergeant Stewart McPherson who won a VC at bloody Lucknow in 1857 during the Indian Rising. There are many stones for farmers (sock and culter) and hammermen (the metalworkers, who of course made guns). In the middle of the top wall there's a very clear crown and hammer stone. A butcher's stone shows his cleavers, a gardener's crossed spade and rake. In the far doorway there's one for a mason's showing compass and square. Go through to see Abbey House, dating to 1608 but often ruined and rebuilt. At one time it was home to the 10th Earl of Dundonald, Thomas Cochrane, the naval genius.

The road goes on inland to the A985 but we'll make our acquaintance with it all too often, shortly.. Walk down again to the Cross and take the Mid Causeway. It has very clear slabs on the higher central part with the rest rough cobbles. This allowed the gentry to keep 'the croun o' the causey' while others walked in the filth at the sides. Note the house at the foot is the local power substation.

Culross to North Queensferry gives a dozen miles of mainly hard-surface walking. Options for continuing. 1. Just turn left to wend on through the twisty main road. Modern houses are built to blend in comfortably. The Red Lion and Primary School are passed and then walk through the carpark to rejoin the FCP. 2. From the Green go through the gates at the pier and take the slim path between railway and sea (not the option for a big storm at high tide). Both options end at the gated railway crossing leading to the big bulge into the Forth of the fenced-off Valleyfield lagoons. The FCP cuts across the neck of this, parallel to the railway (woods on the right) and, after about a mile, crosses the railway by a tubular bridge with long ramps.

The curious traveller however should walk round the lagoons and see the historic remains (industrial archaeology) of Preston Island. The route lies outside a high fence, on the left, throughout, and the lagoons are not visible and, indeed, I've not seen them shown with any agreement on all the maps I've studied. But what are the lagoons?

Preston Island, once offshore, was the site of historic coal shafts and salt pans, an industry that died out in the early nineteenth century. It now sits in a big green landscape (well, one with these lagoons within it), the reclamation material being the ash from Longannet Power Station which was mixed with water and piped along, the new land eventually covered with coal shale and then topsoil to create this unique feature with habitats of meadows, scrub, woods, marshes, lagoons, mudflats and the sea, making for a wealth of wildlife. A walk round it is a unique experience.

A broad track heads out seawards (regular seats make appealing picnic stops), at low tide, with mud flats on the Culross side—with Longannet at its most clearly seen beyond. When the track swings eastwards the three bridges come into view with the Pentland Hills beyond. At the end of this straight the route turns inland and heads through to the Preston Island site. The buildings have been carefully conserved and display boards describe what is seen, and its story. Circle the fenced-off site to glean all the information. Sir Robert Preston (b.

1740) made a fortune with the East India Company and other maritime ventures and, like many nabobs, set about building a grand mansion at Valleyfield, the estate grounds designed by Sir Humphrey Repton, and Preston Island almost a bit of swank, to emulate and surpass Bruce with his earlier Moat Pit. (A profit would be pleasing of course.) The venture was short-lived. Pits were sunk and salt produced but, when the George Pit exploded in 1811, killing miners, a decline began and when salt duties were abolished in 1823 (and in Cheshire better salt was being mined far more easily), the industry died all along the Fife coast. (We'll come on other salt sites at Dysart and St Monans.) For a while Preston Island ran an illicit still! Sir Robert lived till 1834, dying aged 94. His extravagant mansion was demolished in 1941.

The nature of our circular walk changes after Preston Island—in its hollow—and, on the right, tree growth cuts off views of the sea. There is one small glimpse of a lagoon on the right. The path keeps by the fence with a service track over to the right; when it enters the main fenced-off area, the path continues on to reach the main access road in to the forbidden site of the lagoons. Cross this (large gates) and on through woodland to come on the ramped bridge over the railway, thus rejoining the FCP.

The bridge leads down to a carpark. Turn right along a path which then swings left to the B9037 (at the Low Valleyfield town sign and Scottish Power's site). Along the road an obelisk appears which recalls the site of the Valleyfield Colliery 1908-1978. The road to High Valleyfield is passed, we cross the Bluther Burn and walk through Newmills. When we go under a bridge (the same old railway) we are in Torryburn, once the port for Dunfermline and exporting the usual mix of coal, salt and stone. Turn off onto a path by the shore (small carpark) and, if it is low tide, you'll see a vast expanse of mudflats. Torry Bay is not only a Local Nature Reserve but a SSSI (Site of Special Scientific Interest) and Fife SPA (Special Protection Area). A display board describes the birdlife and indicates a site notorious from the witch-hunting years.

The Witches Rock out in the bay is covered at high tide and on it were held trials of suspected witches. They were tested on the rock. If they drowned they were innocent, if they survived it had to be the devil's work—so they were burned. Torryburn had a notorious witch-hunting fanatic but so did many of the Fife coastal towns. Many innocent women faced

brutal interrogation and torture before being burnt at the stake
or drowned or crushed to death under boards over which a
horse and cart ran again and again. Between 1563 and 1769 it
is reckoned about 1,500 people died this way. James VI was a
firm believer in witchcraft and personally supervised some of
their trials, including those accused of raising the storm that
endangered the arrival of his queen-to-be from Denmark.
He wrote a book on demonology, a source for Shakespeare's
Macbeth; the play itself was written to 'sook up' to the king.
The last witch to be killed was a woman drowned at Dornoch
in 1727.

Torryburn is the birthplace of two very different natives
who achieved some fame. Robert Louis Stevenson's *A Child's
Garden of Verses*, 1885, was dedicated, in a poem, to Cummy,
aka Alison Cunningham, his devoted nurse through a sickly
childhood, who regaled him with hair-raising stories (in a
broad Fife accent) which were to influence him as a writer
later. She came from Torryburn, as did the captain of the
ill-fated troopship *Birkenhead*, which sailed from Southampton
in 1852, taking reinforcements to the Xhosa wars, but which
ran aground off South Africa. There were 642 passengers,
including women and children, on board. As the ship settled,
Captain Salmond shouted out what would become something
of a catchphrase, 'Women and children first!' And so it was.
The soldiers stood in ranks to take their chances as the ship
went down. There were only 199 survivors.

Keeping close to the sea's edge we rather bypass Torryburn. Look back to see Longannet and the oil complex across
at Grangemouth. We are very much still aware of the Forth
as river; estuary lies beyond the bridges—today's lowest
bridging point. Cycle track continues ahead, FCP turns up
inland, a steep ascent in woods, then farm track, then road
to meet the shock of the A985. This diversion is necessitated
by a Ministry of Defence/Royal Navy presence. Reaching
Crombie, turn right to escape the traffic. Follow FCP signs.
When the road swings left there is a 'Bingo!' of a view over
the river to the long sweep of the Pentland Hills.

The church in Crombie was built in the 1920s by the Admiralty, which hints at something. A once-busy harbour would
be commandeered by the MoD and used as an armaments depot. I discovered this myself when setting up a bivouac during
a canoe trip of the Forth from source to Kinghorn. I needed to
catch a 04.00 tide so kipped outside this wired-off area that

had a good jetty for launching. I was woken by flashing lights held by men in uniform with an Alsatian dog. 'What the ----- was I doing at the high explosives depot?' Incidentally, when I canoed past Rosyth that night I paddled through among the anchored warships of a NATO exercise—unchallenged.

Our bypass becomes a track leading back to the A985 for another mile-long stretch of road-roar, and a welcome sign for Charlestown and Limekilns. The Scottish lime centre is passed on the left. When the road swings left at the Charlestown road sign do a quick right, left, to follow a path (the Shell Road) down to the harbour and limekilns, the latter the largest and most dramatic in Scotland, at their peak in the eighteenth century and closed in 1956. A good display board describes the industry.

As with Bruce at Culross, here it was Charles, 5th Earl of Elgin, who created a new industry. He laid out the village that bears his name. Their mansion, Broomhall, behind the village, was filled with treasures from Europe. And didn't the 10th Earl bring back some marbles? There was a five-mile tramway to bring down the coal and lime to the kilns on the edge of the harbour. Salt pans were also in the Elgin portfolio. Stone was exported too. The lime was needed for the building boom and also for the 'improving' of agriculture.

Continuing, we pass the road up to Charlestown to join the Promenade into Limekilns. Up on a knoll is a war memorial with sensitive wording. Limekilns is the prettiest upper

Limekilns below Charlestown.

Limekilns village.

reaches village. There's a good green area by the harbour with sheltered seating, and a symbolic fire beacon. The FCP keeps to the shore (the road swings left) with a diversion for the Forth Cruising Club, passes the Sea Scouts base and wends round the sandy bay of Bruce Haven, with its backing of gabions. Don't take the Windylaw Path, an old coffin road, but continue on to the ruins of Rosyth Auld Kirk. There's not much to see but in the far top right corner there are two trade stones with the symbols of hammerman and farmer.

There's a steep pull up initially and then the path swoops on to once more join the A985. The diversion this time is for the Rosyth Dockyard which now looms to the right with the huge crane that was created for the work on the two giant aircraft carriers, *Queen Elizabeth* and *Prince of Wales*. The site was acquired in 1903 and has had its ups and downs ever since.

Ignore Hilton Road to continue for a last stretch of A985 and then turn right (FCP signs) onto a path which will take us into Rosyth, which is reached at the Rosyth Football Club grounds. This is now Wilson Way. Turn left when it meets a bigger carriageway, cross to the other side and on to a big roundabout. Head straight on, now on Ferrytoll Road, to pass Europark (a business park) with its wavy blue-coloured fence. Turn right through its entrance and skirt the carpark until a sign for a Heritage Trail. Go down this through woodland to where there's a board describing the nearby doocot, an unusual one with crow-step gables; worth a look. There are 1,500 nest holes. We then come on a major road which we follow, left, but you might like to see the old Rosyth Castle first. It lies in view across the road, behind trees, a stark fifteenth-century tower. The date 1651 and initials MR (Maria Regina) indicate a Mary Queen of Scots connection. Once it stood on a sea rock reached by a causeway. Cromwell's mother was supposedly born here! His troops partially destroyed it in 1651. Reach it by a diversion right and left, then return to walk along the big Milne Road, straight on at a roundabout and right at traffic lights to gain the B981. We go up under the Queensferry Crossing approach road. The FCP unimaginatively just takes this down to North Queensferry but there are views of, and interests with, the three bridges to divert the curious.

Turn up left to the Double Tree Hotel (by Hilton) and go round it on the right to a viewpoint balcony. 'Wow!' From there continue down steps to pass under the Forth Road Bridge approach road and then more steps down to the road (steps head up to gain the east side of the Forth Road Bridge). Cross, and shortly take the path (kissing gate) right to make your way down below the road bridge and the huge anchor blocks for the cables, to end at the shore with perhaps the best of all views of the Queensferry Passage bridge. Several 'Wows!' Poignantly, there is a walled bench where you can sit and admire bridge and river (and even Longannet; couldn't we keep that landmark, a memorial to a past?). Here is a monument to a worker, John Grant Cousin, the only person to be killed in the bridge's construction, erected by his workmates.

Head up the road to rejoin the Queensferry road again. Come to white houses on the left (note the sundial and lintel with TB 1771). Opposite is a footpath sign. Take it down steps, with Willie's Well behind a grill, to come on the West Bay with seats and a view to the two road bridges. Continuing we come out onto Main Street, the Ferrybridge Hotel opposite, perhaps a good place to stop; welcome to North Queensferry.

Each of the three bridges was a wonder in its day and, with a railway engineer grandfather, I must describe them

The Forth Bridge.

and will do so in historical order: Forth Bridge, Forth Road
Bridge, Queensferry Crossing.

The Rail Bridge is still one of the most visually stunning
bridges ever built. When constructed, sailing ships would
be passing below its cantilevered spans. Originally work
had started to a design by Sir Thomas Bouch, but when
his Tay Bridge blew down in 1879 with the loss of 75 lives
parliament cancelled the project. (The 'floating railway' ferry
from Burntisland which the bridge would replace had been
his very successful brainchild.)

Benjamin Baker designed the present masterpiece with
William Arrol the contractor. Baker's career began as an apprentice in a South Wales ironworks, and he had worked on
Victoria Station in London, was a partner with John Fowler
in creating the city's underground system and helped bring
Cleopatra's Needle from Egypt to the Thames embankment. Workaholic Arrol had already built bridges over the
Wear, Thames and Nile. Fowler took the first railway over
the Thames (Pimlico Bridge) and built St Enoch's station in

Glasgow. Baker became his assistant, then partner and finally took on the Forth Bridge responsibility.

Up to 5000 men took seven years to built the bridge, the first to use steel throughout and, at the time, the biggest-ever man-made structure. Not everyone admired the bridge. John Ruskin loathed it and one book thought it crude and suggested towers and finials be added and gilt paint be applied to its length.

One of the few examples of big being beautiful, the bridge has impressive material statistics: 54,160 tons of steel, 740,000 cubic feet of granite, 48,400 of other stone, 64,300 of concrete, 21,000 tons of cement and 6½ million rivets. There is an area of 145 acres to paint regularly, taking a team of 20 about 4-6 years and 17 tons/7000 gallons of paint. Thatcherite savings saw rapid deterioration, so remedial work kept the bridge under wraps for some years. The notion of starting at one end and working to the other, over and over again, is a myth but the work is exacting, the worker often literally hanging on with one hand and painting with the other. During construction Baker saw a hole pierced through a four-inch timber by a dropped spanner. Throwing lucky pennies out of the train is not a good idea. One worker escaped injury dramatically when

Workers on the Railway Bridge.

a spanner, falling 100 metres, went down inside his waistcoat
and out of his trousers. The bridge's present coating of paint
is designed to last 20 to 25 years. There are plans to create a
public viewing platform on top of the north tower.

The three cantilever towers stand on platforms called cais-
sons: 400 ton, 70 ft. diameter wrought-iron cylinders which
were constructed at Queensferry and floated out. On site,
concrete was poured into them till they sank to the bottom. A
7 ft. space was left at the bottom, kept dry by compressed air,
and the workers cut away the seabed below their feet to reach
the final sturdy base. This area was then filled with concrete
too and steel bedplates affixed to the top so the work on the
superstructure could start. (On the Road Bridge the sheer
weight of the south tower caisson sank it through the boulder clay of the river-bed.) The three towers worked up and
outwards till the spreading arms met. On a hot summer day
the bridge can expand by 8 feet. The bridge is 1.6 miles long
and stands 361 feet above high water level. Two tracks cross
it, and such is its strength that it copes still with 200 modern
trains a day crossing at speeds up to 50 mph. Edward VII, as
Prince of Wales, opened the bridge in 1890. It cost £3 million.
Fife's current logo portrays the Forth Bridge. Though it does
not appear in John Buchan's book, two films of *The 39 Steps*
couldn't resist setting an episode on the bridge.

The loss of life was small for the period: 57. Baker lost no
men under the sea, for instance, yet 119 of 600 employed on
the Brooklyn Bridge had the bends, 16 fatally, while a caisson
in St Petersburg sank onto 28 men with fatal results. Look well
then at this masterpiece of masterpieces.

If the rail bridge did not exist the 1½ mile **Forth Road Bridge**
would have enjoyed greater fame I'm sure. When built, it was
the largest suspension bridge in Europe and the fourth largest
in the world. The central span is 3,300 ft. long with 1,340 ft. side
spans, a southern approach of 1,437 ft. and a northern of 842 ft.
and deep cuttings. The cables were made of 12,000 galvanised
steel wires, each able to bear 100 tons; 314 wires made one
strand and 37 strands one cable. The towers reach 512 feet. In
all, 39,000 tons of steel and 150,000 cubic feet of concrete were
used. Cost: £19.5 million (and 7 lives). Fifteen million vehicles
once crossed the bridge each year. Its historic and aesthetic
status has led to the bridge receiving 'Listed' status.

The earliest record of a crossing here is documented at the
time Queen Margaret died. This refugee princess married

The Forth Road Bridge from the viewpoint.

Malcolm Canmore and was an early commuter between Dunfermline and Edinburgh. The Queen was deeply devout and influential and was canonised in 1250 by Pope Innocent IV; hence an alternative start of the Fife Pilgrim Way from here. The crossing became the Queen's Ferry, as did the town on the Lothian side. The Fife landing was just North Ferry till last century. Storms and strong currents could make crossings hazardous, as Alexanders I and III were to find, and Charles II was to complain at the tolls. The opening of the bridge by the Queen in 1964 brought an end to 800 years of ferry use,

The Queensferry Crossing (R. Cormack).

which was frustrating latterly with nearly a million vehicles a year crossing, but it was fascinating to watch the construction from the ferry queue over 7 years.

On a windy day, if walking, the bridge seems to sway. In fact, it does, by intent, anything up to 22 feet in big gales. (Motorists seldom notice anything then, except a speed restriction.) One construction worker survived falling 180 feet into the sea. Fatalities since have been from road accidents, or suicide jumps (not publicised to discourage copycat attempts). One mystery remains. After blasting, a shaft at the south end was closed for six weeks, and when re-opened a dead sailor was found inside. The bridge has the lighting, drainage, surfacing, maintenance and financial complexities of a small town, and work, as on the Rail Bridge, never stops. Traffic on the bridge is now restricted to pedestrians, cyclists and buses (at commuter times bus travel is quicker than by car).

There was a bit of a panic when it was found that the Forth

Road Bridge's suspension wires were corroding (rusting), a deterioration that questioned the bridge's strength and long-term viability. The problem was eventually brought under control but the bridge was ageing and coping with a workload far beyond what was envisaged, so, after much discussion, a decision was made to build a new bridge (a tunnel was not practical). Thus we have today's wonder, which not only looks good but incorporates the best of modern technology, like features to cope with the wicked winds that sweep the river. A public poll came up with the name **The Queensferry Crossing**. And there she stands. Please sit and look at her. This wonderful web spans 1.7 miles (2.7km), making it the longest three-tower, cable-stayed bridge in the world. The road deck is 180 feet (55m) above the sea. I was lucky enough to sit and watch the very last piece of decking being lifted into place on the Fife shore. The bridge opened in 2017. More statistics: it's the longest free-standing balanced cantilever in the world, the towers are the highest of any British bridge (683ft, 207m; that's 48 double-decker buses one on top of the other). Living east of the bridge I often see the trio in early sunlight and that is the time to see them. For a treat, walk the older bridge one early sunny morning and see the Queensferry's cabling then hang white as lacework.

The bridges truly astonish: each so different, each constructed in a different century, each becoming an icon in turn (there should be some collective noun for such). The Queensferry Crossing was opened by the Queen 53 years to the day after she had opened the Forth Road Bridge.

22

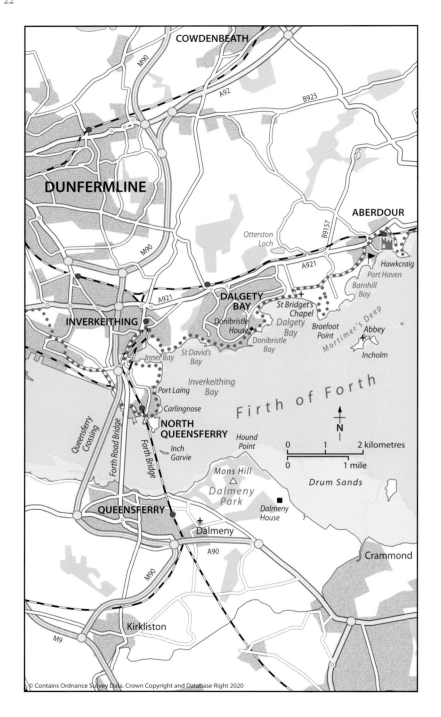

II
Forth Bridge to Burntisland
by Inverkeithing – Dalgety Bay
– Aberdour

O.S. 65, 66/367

North Queensferry. Note the attractive Post Office Lane on
the left as you walk down North Queensferry's main street.
Facing the Albert Hotel the date 1693 is on what was the
Black Cat Inn. Thomas Peastie and Bessie Craich have their
initials above a window. (Genealogists, in Scotland, are given
a help by lintels and gravestones always giving the wife's
original surname.) Next to the Albert Hotel is a rather good
1990 gap-site building. At the slip turning area is a hexagonal
building with a domed light and a flue indicating the light was
originally oil-fired. The last, castellated house above the slip
was once the ferry offices, called Mount Hooly, an obsolete
word for canny or slow, which is how the masons worked!
The officials sat at an octagonal table so no one person had
precedence. Forth Sea Safaris operate from the slip in summer.
Victoria and Albert landed at the Town Pier in 1842, hence the
hotel name. Behind it is the Cadgers' Slip where the cadgers
(carters) met the fishing boats. In the mid-nineteenth century
there were 13 pubs to cater for ferry traffic.

Walk back and turn right past the hotel and follow Battery
Road round till you are below the bridge—Meccano writ
large—beside one of its great towers. Terns may be diving
in summer and seals are often spotted.

The island straddled by the bridge is Inchgarvie, still bris-
tling with old defences. When the Picts defeated the Angles
at the Battle of Athelstaneford the Anglian king's head was
stuck up on a spear on the island as a warning not to cross
the Forth. Burntisland, Inchgarvie and Rosyth were forts
which were a thorn in the flesh to Cromwell, but eventually
he won a battle at Inverkeithing and Scotland fell to his rule.
Ironically, his mother was a Rosyth Stuart.

Head back but take a path to the right signed 'Chapel Place
leading to Helen Place'. The 600-year-old chapel dedicated
to the patron saint of travellers is on the left, access locked

to prevent vandalism. Many sailors and ferrymen are buried in the cemetery and they added the wall round the site as a plaque indicates. 'This is done by sailers in North Ferrie 1752'. One stone inside is inscribed, 'Now here we lay at anchor/ With many of our fleet/ In hopes to weigh at the last day/ Our Admiral Christ to meet.'

Turn right at narrow Helen Place. The cottage at the end, village school till 1827, was called the Malinkie. Turn right at the Malinkie gable and right at the road if going down to visit the Deep Sea World, one of Fife's most popular attractions. If just continuing turn left at the Malinkie and then left again to walk up Post Office Lane.

Deep Sea World was set up in 1993 to make use of the old Battery Quarry which provided the million-gallon aquarium 'tank' through which visitors travel to see the wonders of the deep. There are exhibitions, and audio-visual presentations, facilities for education use and a large café. The Battery Quarry opened in 1764 and its whinstone was used in the bridge's foundations, the Forth and Clyde Canal, Leith Docks, London streets, and exported to the Low Countries and even Russia. Sea water flooding stopped production in 1924. The Battery itself was set up on the crags above following the raid on the Forth by John Paul Jones in 1799. Barrage balloons and guns successfully spoiled raids through both World Wars. Hitler was so depressed at the failure he had pictures faked to show the bridge had been hit.

If returning from Deep Sea World, backtrack under the bridge to Post Office Lane and, through it, turn right to the crossroads with a cluster of wells and the signposting for the FCP. Most obvious is the 1816 Waterloo monument in the shape of a Napoleon's hat. A standard Victorian well stands above, painted black, then there is a plaque on another closed well which shows Europa and the Bull and what looks like a village lassie having a stushie with a foreign sailor—as no doubt occurred at a busy well. (Up the steep brae there's a Jubilee Well—and note the outside stairs on the houses on the left.) A gentle three miles takes us to Inverkeithing.

The FCP rises to pass under the railway and round Carlingnose Point, a SWT Wildlife Reserve, with splendid views to the bridge. The *Witch's Nose* has uncommon flowers like bloody cranesbill, field gentian and dropwort. Fulmars have taken to nesting here and in other places along our walk. An open area is backed by a big quarry. Out to sea there is a

*In the bay, Port Lairg, the white houses of St David's
in the distance.*

remnant pier. Keep to seaward paths or road to drop down
and round to the bay of Port Laing.

Port Laing is a small, sandy bay tucked in under Carlingnose, whose heights once held batteries with barracks on the
bay. There's a duelling stone marking where a Captain Gurley
was killed in 1824 by a Mr Westall after they'd squabbled over
a gambling debt. The latter had to flee the country.

A track wends up to reach North Queensferry station but
we continue on past three smart houses which have spilled
down onto the bay itself. From the far end of the bay the path
weaves on to pick up another small access road. The view to
the estuary opens out and the white 'clean-gleaming' houses
of St David's Harbour stand out. The Inverkeithing inlet remains hidden for a while, though the piers, old and new, on
the other side look so near. Round a bend—and all is revealed.
Oddly the two arms of the inlet are called East Ness and West
Ness though they lie north and south of each other.

There is something of a shock to suddenly come on busy
(often noisy) industry: the Inverkeithing Scrap Terminal, now
almost hidden behind high walls, outside of which we make
our way. The site was originally Ward's shipbreaking yard. I
can recall a huge carrier, the *Implacable*, being cannibalised in
1955 and the proud *Mauretania* in 1965. The hall of the office
building was decorated with the name-plates of scores more:

Revenge, Royal Sovereign, Rodney, Majestic. This last was actually German in origin but was a trophy of World War I. Changed from *Bismarck* to *Majestic* (sounds like a hotel!), she was once the largest liner operating. There was overcapacity following the Cunard/White Star merger and *Majestic* was delivered here for scrapping. However, with Hitler's war looming, the Royal Navy took her as a training ship, renamed HMS *Caledonia* and based at Rosyth. There was something of a panic when the war began and she was beached, went on fire and so ended in Ward's after all. It took several years to dismantle the ship. Now scrap has replaced shipbreaking. Industry constantly changes, for we've just walked along a one-time railway to Cruickness, piers decay, transport changes, and gone completely are the salt-pans, woodyard, limekiln and bonemill. On the left, when we exit to carparks and roads, lies the vast Cruicks Quarry, the only one locally still operating. Begun in 1828, its stone still goes all over Britain and abroad. Most recently barges took stone for strengthening the sea defences at Dysart, the Wemyss villages and the railway embankment above Pettycur sands. The scale doesn't really show from here; the central hole goes far below sea level. Pennant on his travels noted quarrying in this area in the nineteenth century. Only the quarry names survive now: Ferry Toll, Welldean, Lucknow, Jubilee, Battery etc. At the start of last century a quarryman, working a 10-hour day, earned £1 for his labours.

Continue under an abandoned railway to turn right at the main road (Hope Street). Walking on we pass an Episcopal church which looks like an alpine chapel, a house (with elephant gates) which calls itself Niravaana, some allotments, St Peter in Chains church, Scout hall and then a more imposing front with a date, MDCCCXXXIII, which challenges interpretation. **Inverkeithing** is a very old town with some surviving buildings worth seeing.

Off right is the friary, now the local museum, in the *hospitium* of a Grey Friars Monastery dating back to the fourteenth century. Behind are gardens in what would have been the cloisters. Next to it is the town's Civic Centre, a multi-purpose building with local information, displays, library, café etc. Gardens behind it as well.

Continue along the wide High Street, passing the Royal Hotel, birthplace of Samuel Greig. He was born in 1735 and died as Grand Admiral of Russia. A schoolboy trip to the Baltic in his father's trading vessel started off his sea career.

He served with Hawke, was at the siege of Havana and volunteered for Russian service. He was largely responsible for destroying the 'invincible' Turkish fleet, then reorganised the Baltic fleet for Catherine the Great, beat off Swedish attacks and built the Kronstadt Fort so well (Carlingnose stone) that Napier's British fleet, 85 years later, found it 'a hard nut to crack'. One son also became a Russian admiral, two others served in the British navy and another was Russian consul in London where he died at the age of 29, and his young widow then married a Dr Somerville, of whom more when we explore Burntisland. Another cousin also made it as a Russian admiral—and so too, did Scots-born Yankee John Paul Jones.

Along a bit, the Burgh Arms (dated 1664-1888), has an attractive sign and another door is dated 1688 with I.B's lintel text: 'God's providence is my inheritance'. Then we come to Bank Street and the gem of the burgh's sixteenth-century mercat cross, vividly painted as it would have been in those days. The shields are of Robert III, Queen Annabella Drummond, Duke of Rothesay and the red heart of the Douglas.

Houses built entirely of stone seldom pre-date the end of the fifteenth century (so not much survives from before that period) but the Fife coast is unusually rich in early stone building such as we see here. A forestair leading to upper-level living areas was a common feature and partly defensive (a stair was an effective defence in pre-gunpowder days) and partly practical (below lay traders' cellars, room for fishermen's nets etc). Crowstep gables allowed beams to be laid across to work on thatch or pantiles, often at too steep a pitch for standing on. The pantiles came from the Low Countries as ballast for the ships trading salt and coal from the Fife coast.

Across Townhill Street lies the fine old town hall or tolbooth which also has an *The Mercat Cross, Inverkeithing.*

An old house in Inverkeithing.

outside stair, coat of arms and so on. Debtors were imprisoned on the top floor beside the 1467 bell, a court room occupied the middle floor and the 'black hole' (prison) lay below. The mercat cross would originally have been nearby and luckenbooths (lockable stalls) and market day activity would echo down the streets.

Turn right once up past the tolbooth onto Church Street, as the High Street has become, to reach the church, the tower of which looks, and is, old (fourteenth-century) and the adjacent graveyard with many of the stones sunk deeply in the ground but full of interest. See if you can add to my tally of trade symbols: weaver (shuttle), sailor (anchor), tailor (scissors), butcher (cleaver), wright (compass and square)... The church hall opposite is in the Fordell Lodging which dates to about 1670 and was the 'town house' of the Hendersons of Fordell.

That really does for exploring Inverkeithing. The railway station lies five minutes walk further along past the church and buses all call at the town centre where there are restaurants, cafés, pubs, chip-shops etc. We'll pick up the route again at the tolbooth. The town's most noted date is 1651: the Battle of Inverkeithing when Cromwell routed the Royalists and soon had Scotland to heel.

From Inverkeithing to Burntisland is an attractive ten miles. From the Tolbooth head down (Townhall Street) then turn right (Port Street) to descend to a footbridge over a railway. Rather than head off along Preston Crescent opposite, walk along the road to where the Keithing Burn becomes a sea inlet—with a new view of the new bridge. Cross a footbridge to the large reclaimed green open area, Ballast Bank, and follow its seaward edge. Inverkeithing Harbour now only has a few pleasure boats, but at one time a waggonway from Halbeath, near Dunfermline, brought coal down for shipping abroad.

There's a clear view over to the scrapyard. Sporting and play areas and Leisure Centre take us to the far corner, to pick up the FCP by the big shed.

We soon come on the huge Prestonhill Quarry, the empty heart filled with water, its derelict pier fretworking out to sea. The path leads us on round to St David's Bay. **Dalgety Bay** (the town) was only created in the 1960s but now invades down to St David's Harbour and inland to the A921 coast road by the Donibristle and Hillend industrial estates. The town is attractive but no more Scottish than Margate. We skirt most of its amoebic sprawl.

The harbour at St David's Bay was built in 1752 to export coal from the Fordell mines inland, the coal being brought down along wooden rails, drawn by horses (as at Inverkeithing)—Fife's first 'railway'. Fordell Castle was the home of the one-time exotic MP, Sir Nicholas Fairbairn. The harbour serviced minesweepers in the war, Donibristle had a naval base and HMS *Cochrane*, while every prominence had its defences because of the Forth Bridge.

The St David's Harbour development is stylish with a touch of the vernacular in red roofs and harling. A curve of bay leads to the village green facing the remnant of harbour and with a big anchor much loved of children at play. For the next stretch paths and roads alternate as the coastline is followed. The luxury houses enjoy magnificent views up-river and over to Hound Point, an oil terminal where tankers can load a million gallons of Grangemouth-refined oil in 24 hours. The continuation has been much improved by the volunteer Community Woodland Group. Steps dip to Hopeward Wood. On a crisp February day this proved a rich birding area with all the garden birds, mobs of blackbirds, goldfinch, speugs (sparrows), siskins, greenfinch, a blackcap, a yaffle (green woodpecker) undulating ahead and a din of shore calls from gulls, crows, eiders, redshanks, curlews and oystercatchers. Steps lead up to reach Bathing House Wood, with Downing Point jutting out into the firth and offering the best panorama of the day, then steps descend. Do visit this site, marked with dual WW2 gun emplacements. The point seems to aim straight at Inchcolm with the Bass Rock on the horizon and, closer, to the pencil of the Oxcars light on its rock right in the centre of the shipping channel, between Inchcolm (N) and the Cow and Calves and Inchmickery (S). It was one of the last 'rock' lights built, in 1886.

Keep along the bay with its 'superior housing'. When the way on is blocked, a path detours round the shoreside houses briefly. It is worth making a brief detour out and back, left, through the rook-loud Chapel Wood to see Donibristle chapel. This was completed as an Episcopal chapel in 1732 and is the family vault of the Morays. At least nine earls are thought to be buried within. The twelfth Earl of Moray was reputedly seven feet tall, and the find of an eight-foot coffin seems to confirm this. The west face bears a fine coat of arms.

The seaside is regained to walk along below the old Donibristle House site, now restored as luxury flats and with the magnificent historic iron entrance gateway setting off the balanced splendour.

Donibristle House has had a chequered history. Its first mention is in the twelfth century, when it was the residence of the Abbot of Inchcolm. An Earl of Moray was the illegitimate son of James V and so half-brother to Mary Queen of Scots, but best known is his grandson, the Bonnie Earl o' Moray of the song. After he fell foul of James VI, the Earl of Huntly and his cronies fired the house and murdered those escaping. (The murdered earl's son was later to marry the murderer's daughter!) That fire was in 1592. In 1790 the west wing of a new house went up in flames, and in 1858 the main house burnt down. In 1912 the shell was pulled down leaving the two wings. An underground passage linked them with cellars and kitchens so spacious they could garage several double decker buses. The west wing went on fire in 1985. The site was used by the navy in the war, was later the estate office and is now the heart of the luxury housing development. I hope they have adequate fire insurance.

Donibristle House.

We round to come in sight of another small harbour. Here Robert Moffat, the famous missionary and father-in-law of David Livingstone, nearly lost his life when pulling a fellow worker from the sea. He was then working in the gardens of the big house. Overlooking the bay is the pleasing conversion of the old stable block. Note the circular windows and gateway: Donibristle horses were better housed than the estate workers.

Keep inland to pass Dalgety Bay Sailing Club, and return to the shore of Dalgety Bay itself, bird-loved mud flats at low tide, onto which it is not advisable to venture (radioactivity!). The walk is pleasant, with Inchcolm now nearer and the mix of mud and woodland, marsh, fields and gardens gives a wide variety of wildlife. (On one walk I heard woodpecker, blue tit, kestrel and eider all at once—while watching a treecreeper.) We follow round the bay (Crowhill Wood) a wide path to **St Bridget's Chapel**.

The miniature house at the wall is a watch house. Watch-houses were common in early Victorian days when raiding body-snatchers were selling corpses to the anatomists. The burn by the entrance was fed through basins so horses could be refreshed after their long trek to the chapel.

St Bridget's is a delight, and old, receiving its charter in 1178. Post-Reformation lairds built 'lofts' or 'aisles' (private pews in side wings) and one, upstairs, the Dunfermline Aisle, is a suite reached by a winding stair. There are some rare

By St Bridget's Chapel.

seventeenth-century stones and others of interest. The first on the right, entering the grounds, commemorates the drowning of a Liverpool lad of 13 in a 1799 shipwreck in the Forth. The bell is now in Aberdour Church and has the un-Presbyterian inscription: 'O mother of God remember me'. Note how some of the stones declare how many 'lairs' (spaces) are taken up. My favourite item is the table stone east of the church, where the corner scrolls are grinning faces.

From the church head up and take the first road, right (SROW sign for Braefoot). The FCP takes a less-interesting detour inland. Heading along, don't be tempted by a branch turning down right: it leads to the local sewage works. When the big woods are reached, turn off for a worthwhile diversion, signposted for Braefoot Point. The interest lies in the remains of wartime defences. A small rail line came out from a magazine and ran out to big gun emplacements. (Test firing shattered windows across the water in Leith!) An incline went up to anti-aircraft sites and balloon anchorages. Wander on seawards and circle left to see Braefoot and Inchcolm, a view all the better (as many are on the coast) when the trees are bare in winter.

Inchcolm now lies close offshore, across Mortimer's Deep, which allows supertankers of up to 300,000 tons to nestle into the Braefoot terminal below us. The oil is pumped up to Mossmorran's huge Star Wars petro-chemical site 6km. inland. Ethylene gas is pumped onto tankers for export. Standing on top of the abbey tower on Inchcolm once, I watched a supertanker berth and the ship's bridge was more or less on the same level. The point gives great views and I'll add notes on Inchcolm.

Inch is just another Gaelic-originated Scots word for *island* with the Forth Estuary and Loch Lomond having popular clusterings of the word. Inchcolm is Columba's Isle, Colm being another form of the saint's name. One of the island's earliest (true) incidents has a mention in Shakespeare's *Macbeth*: Sueno, defeated by Macbeth at Kinghorn, is allowed to bury his dead on Inchcolm—for a big fee. A strange hogsback grave dates to that period.

The island is famous for its abbey, which has survived better than most, its island setting being a defence both against attack and the pillaging of its stones (think of St Andrews cathedral!) Alexander I was caught in a storm crossing the Forth in 1123 and vowed, if saved, to found an abbey in St Columba's name. His craft reached the island and he was provided for by a hermit who lived in a cell, a 'desert' (from which the name Dysart), which still survives. David I (Alexander's brother) founded a priory which became an abbey a century later. Sir William Mortimer, Aberdour landowner, fell out with the monks but nevertheless gave half his lands and an endowment to ensure he was buried on the holy island. Somehow, on the crossing, his lead coffin went overboard; hence the name Mortimer's Deep off from here.

Columba's name was obviously one to be respected. English raiders in 1335 bore off abbey treasures, only to be overtaken by a storm off Inchkeith, so they pleaded with the saint for mercy, promising restitution. The storm abated and they landed the pillaged goods at Kinghorn. Another raid

Inchcolm over the Braefoot Terminal.

Inchcolm Abbey.

penetrated to the Ochils and went off with Dollar church goods. Not having interceded with the saint the ship sank in Mortimer's Deep—and Dollar parish church was dedicated to St Columba. English incursions were of a more serious nature during Henry VIII's 'Rough Wooing', when the monks evacuated the vulnerable island and, soon after, the Reformation brought its end, the last old monk dying in 1578. The abbey however is the most complete ruin of its kind in Scotland (Edinburgh's tolbooth was made from its stolen masonry). In 1854 workers found a skeleton standing upright within a wall of the Abbot's House.

Several times, like Inchkeith, the island was used as a convenient quarantine station. Before modern times infectious diseases were rightly feared. In 1845 a fleet visit of the Russian navy of Czar Nicholas I saw many sailors left there to die of a fever. About 1582 the *William of Leith* brought plague from England and was banished to the island, where most of the crew perished. Excavations have found huge numbers of interments.

Many ruins are obviously dating to World War II (and some to World War I, or the Napoleonic period) and the best viewpoint, up on the eastern end, is one such site, with a clear prospect over the island and the pretty abbey. During World War II a boom was stretched from Inchcolm across to Cramond Island on the Lothian shore. All the *inches* were heavily armed, like static warships anchored in the firth.

Inchmickery's buildings were intentionally made to look like a warship.

Do make sure of climbing to the top of the abbey tower (which had its upper floors as a doocot) though those of noble girth will find it a bit of a squeeze. A rare thirteenth-century mural painting has been discovered in the chancel, showing a procession of robed figures, censers swinging, though sadly the top section (with their heads) is missing. The island is green and pleasant, with little bays and quiet corners, and time seems to slow down to reward the visitor. Summer sailings allow access and Inchcolm is in the care of Historic Scotland.

The island offers good exploratory walking, interesting flowers, nesting gulls and often seasonal rafts of puffins offshore. There is a Visitor Centre (facilities) and a Historic Scotland custodian.

Wander back along the spine of the headland, the works just below, then cut back to the entrance. Continue round the bend in the road till at the start of the oil site, then turn left up a straight, fenced path, between fields, to reach a small road. Turn right at the road which is lined with daffodils in season, as is all the route ahead to Aberdour. A pedestrian underpass takes us below the Braefoot terminal road.

The Field Path from Braefoot Point.

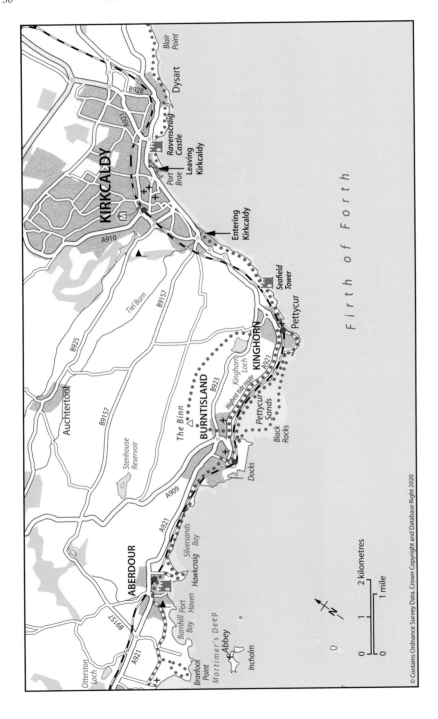

Continuing, St Colm's House is off right, with Downan's Plantation a mass of snowdrops in February. Shoreward is a golf course with the Bell Rock jutting into the Forth with Aberdour Bay and the Hawkcraig beyond.

The big mast away ahead stands on the Binn. The nearer obelisk stands on Cuttle Hill and was built by the Mortons in 1744 as a landmark they could pick out from their estate at Dalmahoy in Midlothian. Our avenue reaches **Aberdour** at a set of very fine sun gates. The Woodside Hotel opposite has a bearded face on a lintel which is claimed to be of Admiral Sam Greig. As it was previously Grey's Hotel it is probably just of the original hotelier. A dominie was also a Greig. The Norwegian composer originally spelt his name the Scots way and was of Scottish descent.

If into doocots turn left, and after 250m., on the left you'll see an unusual round 'lectern' doocot. On the way back, behind a wall, is a standard 'lectern' doocot. (It's by a house with a forestair and 1713 lintel.) Both are on private property, so just look! Head on east again; there isn't much of Aberdour really, originally two villages pushed to the edges of Moray and Morton estates and split by the Dour Burn. Walk on to the 1910 Spence Memorial clock (he was a long-serving G.P.). Look round to the right to see the seventeenth-century Aberdour House, once the Morton home, now restored as the centrepiece of a more sensitive housing estate. Before that the Mortons lived in their castle of Aberdour. Two minute's walk (inland) lies a 'Sensitive' Garden. In 1990 Aberdour Station won the Best Kept Station in Britain award, and the Scottish title eleven years in a row. The signal box is now a studio. Ways to reach the castle are clearly signed.

Robert the Bruce granted **Aberdour Castle** to his nephew Thomas Randolph after Bannockburn, but he sold it to a Douglas in whose ownership it remained as they clawed up to being earls. This was no sinecure: the Regent Morton—for the infant James VI—had his head cut off by the guillotine nicknamed the Maiden, which is in the Museum in Edinburgh to this day. Another Earl of Morton imprisoned Mary Queen of Scots in Loch Leven Castle. His eldest son never succeeded, as he was captured by Barbary pirates and the Civil War nearly ruined them. The original tower is ruinous now but the eastern ranges survive. However it is the setting and details that interest. There are three sundials, one from Aberdour house ('A Roman altar standing on four cannon balls'), one in

The beehive doocot at Aberdour Castle.

the walled garden, and one up on the wall, cut into a corner
to maximise the possible sunlight hours. The castle became
a monastery for the filming of *Outlander*.

The gem is a well-preserved 'beehive' doocot, one you can
actually see inside. There are about 600 nesting boxes, and
a revolving structure of ladders (a 'patence') allowed access
to the boxes (the base can be seen in the centre of the floor),
for pigeon was an important part of the diet for the well-off
who alone were allowed a doocot. The pigeons ate the poor
folks' grain, of course! The string courses circling the outside
gave the birds a perch, but the overhang stopped rats from
entering. This doocot is sixteenth-century. Several others will
be seen on our walk, Fife having been rich in 'bunnet lairds'.
Beehive doocots were superseded by lectern-shaped doocots,
which are quite common, usually rectangular with a single
pitched roof and crowstep gables for the birds to perch on
and, always, anti-rat courses. When fancier doocots were built
that was the one feature kept, and always indicates a doocot.

The castle is in the care of Historic Scotland, and there's a
tearoom which may be welcome. From the walled garden with
its herbaceous borders and central sundial, a gate in the east
wall leads out to Hawkcraig Road, just at the drive into the

church, our next place to visit. If the gate is locked, go back to the entrance drive for a gate into the station carpark from which, right, a footpath leads through to Hawkcraig Road. Inland of this trim floral station stands a house, Hillside, where another claimant to 'the second-last duel' was fought, between James Stuart of Hillside and Alexander Boswell, a son of Johnson's biographer, who was killed.

St Fillan's Church. The drive is lined with old grave-stones, shifted there when the ground level was raised. First note of the church was in 1178, and a healing-well (site now unknown) made it a popular place of pilgrimage. A leper window (a narrow slit so lepers, kept safely outside, could still hear the service) is blocked by a stone addressed to pilgrims. There are some interesting stones. An inverted anchor points to being anchored in heaven. Several have rhymes, like: 'My glass is run / And yours is running / Be feared to sin / For death is coming.' Rev. Robert Blair, a famous Covenanter, is buried here. Does the architecture look a bit strange? Surely the roof is far too big? It almost reaches the ground. The clue is how one descends to the interior. The walls are normal, it's the ground that has risen, being covered with that extra depth of soil so it could continue in use as a graveyard!

Aberdour gravestone: 'Anchored above'.

Carry on down Hawkcraig Road. Local pro-nunciation is probably more accurate with Hawcraig (*hall craig*). When the road swings left into the big car park turn right down a steep path/steps to the harbour. Turn left. There's benches at a viewing spot (good to Inchcolm and Hound Point). At houses and Forth View Hotel turn onto the road but leave it at once up a steep, rough spiralling of steps to reach the green dome of Hawkcraig Point, the cliffs of which are a popular rock climbing ground where the tyro can, sometimes all too literally, make a splash.

Climbers on the Hawkcraig.

Hawkcraig probably offers the most extensive view we have of the upper part of the Forth estuary. The Dour Burn flows out into the Aberdour harbour at the Stone Pier and old pictures show queues of holidaymakers waiting to board paddle steamers. The now-ruined New Pier allowed sailings at low tides and also serviced Inchcolm.

From Hawkcraig continue down by the red and white sea marks to a tarred road. A display board tells the story of HMS *Tarlair*, a hush-hush World War I research station (into underwater detection) which was blessed by having the C in C (Beatty) living in Aberdour House. Walk along to the **Silver Sands**. The name was dreamed up last century by the tourist publicity boys, who almost certainly didn't mention two sewage pipes running out into the bay. Recently the rare sparling, or cucumber-smelt, has re-established itself in the estuary. (A shoal could be noted from the shore by the strong smell of cucumber!) The Silver Sands (a Blue Flag Beach) remains a popular corner in summer and there's a good café.

Aberdour crops up in an old ballad, *Sir Patrick Spens*, which gallops off with 'The king sits in Dunfermline toun, / Drinking the blude-red wine; / "O whar will I get a skeely skipper

/ To sail this guid ship o' mine?" ' The grim result is 'Half ower, half ower, tae Aberdour, / It's fifty fathoms deep? / And thair lies guid Sir Patrick Spens / Wi the Scots Lords at his feet.' This is often taken for the journey to fetch the Maid of Norway to succeed her grandfather Alexander III (of whom more shortly), but she was taken to Orkney where she died, and the king would not have been sending for her as he was obviously alive if looking for the 'skeely skipper'. Alexander III was buried at Dunfermline. Burntisland is twinned with Flekkefjord in Norway, a modern link. (Buckhaven and Methil twin with Swedish Trelleborg and Kirkcaldy and Levenmouth with German towns.)

The path is often on the embankment of the railway (just over the wall) which runs close to the sea through this richly wooded area. A huge beech dominates the path as it goes under railway bridge 54. (Bridges are numbered from Edinburgh.) Some dampness and water leaking onto the path indicates we've hit a limestone area. There's a spout of a spring ('well' in Scots) and then the bigger Starley Burn (by the castellated bridge), which is so high in lime content it was called the Fossil Falls, as objects left in its flow soon coat over with lime. In the middle of last century there were ferocious battles, legal and physical, when the Earl of Morton tried to close the route to the public. A new body (now the Scottish Rights of Way and Access Society, or Scotways) was involved, and only renewed pertinacity by the public prevented the railway succeeding where landowners had failed. It even needed litigation to ensure access to the Hawkcraig and the Silver Sands.

The path runs by the curve of a wall, then joins a corkscrew road which twists down to one-time Carron Harbour. Our path on is along the landward side of the railway. Starley Harbour, to the west, is ruined, but both these were once busy with exporting limestone to Falkirk iron works. There are signs as we walk on of another line that brought stone from Ninelums Quarry.

The next landmark is modern enough: a huge radio mast in the field to the left of our walled way. Across the Forth we are now looking to Edinburgh, a fine silhouette from Castle to Arthur's Seat with the painted backdrop of the Pentlands beyond. (Few capitals have a hill at their hearth and a range at the doorstep.) We twist down to what was, until 2003, almost the most industrialised site of our whole walk, a vast aluminium processing plant—which had nothing to do with

Looking towards Burntisland with the green of reclaimed ground. Inchkeith in the distance.

the town's name, Burntisland being neither burnt nor an island. It could be a corruption of Brunty's Land or such, a *land* being a high building, as on the Royal Mile across the Forth, and Brunty/Brunton someone's name. Originally it was just Wester Kinghorn.

Alumina was extracted from bauxite imported from Ghana and brought into the harbour by barges. The red colouring once tinted the town. Paths were often made from the waste, and the flat green towards the sea here is all reclaimed land which was landscaped in 1982. Burntisland's alumina and dried hydrates went into a hundred different products, from sparkplugs to toothpaste and pottery, to fire retardants and paints. The aluminium works closed in 2002 and the site is now an extensive housing development alongside which we walk. Turn right to go under the railway and pass a pond, to reach the reclaimed area with **Burntisland** up on the slopes ahead. Off right is what was once a tidal mill which worked on high tide filling a reservoir whose water was then used on the ebb to drive the mill. Turn left. At the multiple crossroads cross and take the steps up beside the houses, then turn left up what is Melville Gardens. A small store is passed. At the top, right, are houses in what were once the stables of Rossend Castle (not quite as posh as Donibristle's), dated 1816.

Rossend Castle itself stands off right as our road swings left again (still Melville Gardens) and is an example of what can be done in the way of rescuing a ruin, in this case one with a Mary Queen of Scots story. If every castle seems to claim a Marian visit this is probably true enough: both she and Queen Elizabeth in England regularly quartered the land, staying with their nobles in turn. They had to for economic reasons, and it brought the hosts down a bit and kept an eye on them. In 1563 an over-romantic French courtier, Pierre de Chastelard, was discovered hiding under the queen's bed at Rossend. As he'd already done this at Holyrood Palace it was too much: he was taken to St Andrews where he lost his head in more literal fashion.

The castle was allowed to decay, especially after a seventeenth-century painted ceiling was taken off to the national museum, and the local authority nearly knocked it down. Fortunately it was taken on by a firm of restoration architects with the result we see. What would M. Q. of S. have made of drawing boards and computer screens in her bedroom? Past the castle turn onto the grassy area with big trees (chestnut, beech, old Spanish chestnut) where there's a gazebo (folly)

Rossend Castle.

from which there's a good view down to the harbour, one first noted by Agricola for whom it was *portus gratiae*. The harbour area is now dominated by Briggs Marine, who look after many of the buoys etc round our coast. Cromwell occupied Burntisland in 1657 and built harbour defences. Pepys noted Burntisland being bombarded by the Dutch a decade later. Mary's grandson, Charles I, has less fond memories, crossing here in the *Dreadnought* at the end of his coronation journey, he watched his baggage train and many of his entourage come to grief when the *Blessing of Burntisland* ferry capsized in a sudden squall. The treasure known to have been on board has led to various attempts at locating the wreck. James VI on his only visit north after the union saw a boatload of courtiers drowned in a stormy crossing.

In thick fog (October 1879) a trawler *Integrity* sank after colliding with the ferry *John Stirling*—which picked up the crew. The most scandalous sea disaster locally was the sinking of the record-breaking Cunard liner *Campania*, which had been converted into an aircraft carrier in WWI. Anchored a mile off Burntisland, on 5 November 1918, she snapped her anchor and drifted off to collide with three battleships in turn, *Royal Oak*, *Glorious* and *Revenge*, before the damage sank her. At 18,000 tons she is still the single biggest Forth casualty.

The harbour was famous for having the world's first train ferry (1847) designed by Thomas Bouch of Tay Bridge notoriety. The actual wagons were carried across to Granton, the service eventually giving way to the Forth Bridge in 1890. Shipbuilding turned to building light aircraft carriers during the last war, but shipbuilding failed in 1968. In 1667, 30 Dutch ships threatened shipping in the harbour but were beaten off. They only managed to capture one Leith privateer.Walking on we come on an archway spanning the road. The east side is more interesting with coats of arms dated 1392, 1563 and 1932. The road goes over the coast railway then, shortly after, at an opening, descend beside a car park to reach the west end of the High Street. Rail and port enthusiasts cross to go along Harbour Place and visit the harbour, such as it is (the view back has Rossend Castle perched above) and the stylish station building, a listed building. The Smugglers Inn is old and stands in a row of good restorations. Heading along the High Street, with or without this diversion, note the twin gables (of a pub) across the street, which is the town's oldest building (1671). Walk past the police post for about 30 yards then turn right through a pend with a very fine pair of marriage lintels (rescued during the tasteless 1960s reconstructions) which are dated 1626. Continue up some steps.

Somerville Square comes as quite a surprise. One of the houses has a plaque about **Mary Somerville**, briefly mentioned before as the wife of Samuel Greig, the Russian Grand Admiral. Her father was Sir William Fairfax who fought at Camperdown. Against all the odds of her time and genteel breeding, Mary became a notable scientist (largely self-educated) and had papers published on topics like 'Molecular and Microscopic Science' and 'Mechanics of the Heavens'. As a girl she was fascinated by fossils in the limestone being exported, she taught herself algebra, which led to trouble as the servants complained at her vast use of candles (were they being blamed?). Her parents discouraged her precocity, but she gradually found books and mentors before marrying her cousin and moving to London. He died shortly after and she then married another cousin, an army doctor, who gave her full support. She lived into her nineties. The Oxford college is named after her. She appears on a Scottish £10 banknote. Return from this attractive remnant by the same *pend*.

Back on the High Street you may spot a cross marked in the road—the site of the mercat cross, long gone. The library and one-time town hall (a 1907 Carnegie gift) has a museum upstairs which is worth a visit and has in part been designed as an Edwardian showground or fair, which continues still in the summer on the Links.

Across the street is the renowned Museum of Communications, while turning right onto Kirkgate are the Heritage Trust rooms, both with summer exhibitions. Along, left, spot a commemorative plaque: 'David Danskin. Founder and first captain of Arsenal Football Club. Born near here 9.11.1863'. At the crossroads is Hanselled Books (large secondhand stock).

At the top of the Kirkgate, left, is the famous church, the oldest post-reformation church in Scotland. Vandalism means gates and church are locked, but if you have made contact with the curator you'll enjoy your visit to the most interesting church of the coast.

Building a church was a precondition of James V's charter for the burgh. The church was built all square with pulpit in the centre to emphasise 'the equality of believers' but merchants and members of the crafts' guilds (hammermen, bakers, masons, wrights, etc.,) soon took gallery seats and

Burntisland's historic parish church.

adorned them with their arms, and the laird, of course, had to have a super-ornate pew (later the magistrates' pew). Unwilling to risk plague at St Andrews the General Assembly convened at Burntisland with James VI in attendance, and it was here in 1601 that the translation of the Bible into English was decided: the 400- year-old Authorised or King James version. (The work was somewhat delayed as James VI became James I of England in 1603.) The balcony can also be reached by an outside stair (a Fife feature), being a fishermen's loft, so they could enter and leave without disturbance—presumably the tides, being God's responsibility, allowed for this exemption. Both loft door and main door (1592) have upside-down anchors. The tower was a 1749 addition and the weathervane is a gilded cockerel. There's a notable painted ceiling. The nautical connection is strong, with vivid sailing galleys, battles and navigational instruments shown on the sailors' gallery, and a model of the *Great Michael*.

In the cemetery, right round the back, is the imposing Watson family monument with a horizontal skeleton reclining at

Painting in the Sailors' Gallery, Burntisland Church.

the foot. The back-to-front figure 4 (Ꮞ) is a merchants' symbol, indicating the four corners of the world. There is a monument to an unfortunate cadger (i.e. carrier, the figure with the barrow) who was not quite all there, yet spent his free time, weekdays, visiting the old and sick and giving them the minister's Sunday sermon word for word. He was killed by a student prank which went wrong when they spiked his beer with snuff. In the modern cemetery a stone recalls a slave: 'In loving remembrance of Pete (Petronella Hendrick). Born at Providence, Nickerie, Surinam... For over 60 years the faithful and devoted nurse and friend of the family of Robert Kirke...' The 'big black mama' declined to leave the family (refusing a free passage, etc.), and was remembered locally as 'a cheery buddie wi a guid Fife accent'.

Turn right leaving the church and continue along a narrowing of East Leven Street to pause before a rather ecclesiastical-looking building on the right, the 1854 Parsonage, now flats for the elderly, the work of Rev. George Hay Forbes, an 'Episcopal liturgist and publisher'. Hidden in that dry biography is another extraordinary character. He came to Burntisland, newly ordained, in 1848 and started a school. This soon grew to 90 pupils, so he built this edifice, sometimes dressing ashlars himself, though crippled with what could have been polio. (To assist movement inside he had a rope suspended which he abseiled down, and a speaking tube helped convey messages up the way). Much of his early life was bed-bound, but he learned to speak 20 languages and could read 30 more. A vast Bible translation scheme was undertaken. Ecclesiastes was his portion, translated *and* printed in 41 languages, including Hebrew, Arabic, Ethiopic, Syriac, Peshitto, Persian and Greek. On his arrival the dour people wouldn't help him up when his crutches slipped; 21 years on he was elected provost. For relaxation he'd sit at the rear of a cart, feet dangling, and have it backed into the sea so he could 'paddle'.

East Leven Street comes out at the Links, as the old common is called. In the corner, after we turn left, you'll see a cast-iron 1887 fountain with a cherub under the canopy with the town crest. See if you can find the open-jawed crocodiles on it! There are interesting information boards. Across the end of the High Street is the Old Port pub, which stands where the East Port (gate) once gave entrance to the walled town, a very ornate, two-tone sandstone building. Salamanders flank the door; above, figures hold a shield and, higher again, there is a triple sundial with mottos: 'Time Flies', 'I mark Time, dost thou?', 'I only count the sunny hours'. Looking along you'll see the war memorial which stands at the foot of Cromwell Road. His troops camped on the Links. At the top of Cromwell Road is a large primary school, required because of the houses we passed boosting the population. The school was opened by a young girl named Malala Yousafzai, the activist and human rights campaigner who won the Nobel Peace Prize in 2014. At 17, she is the youngest ever Nobel prizewinner. Burntisland is backed by the Binn (hill) with a big mast on top and is well worth ascending for the panoramic view. The walk is described in Appendix I. Most Burntisland hotels or B & Bs lie along Kinghorn Road, eastwards, back along the High Street, or on Cromwell Road.

III
Burntisland, Kinghorn, Kirkcaldy
O.S. 66, 59 / 367

The **Burntisland Links** is our starting point, but how we go will depend on the tide. Kirkcaldy lies six or seven miles ahead. There is also the option of climbing the Binn, the 193m hill that backs the town and gives a view quite disproportionate to its modest height. The Links themselves are occupied by the shows (travelling fair) in high summer, and the third week in July sees the local Highland Games (when local accommodation may be difficult to find). This activity dates back to the 1651 practice of horse racing (Burntisland-Kinghorn) to keep Cromwell's troops active. The silver cup was competed for till 1812. Cromwell built a fort on the Lammerlaws, the point beyond the obvious modern swimming pool complex (Beacon Centre), which replaced a one-time popular open-air pool. The windy headland was where local criminals were hung. Plague victims in 1608 were 'lodged' on the Links and Hessian troops were billeted in 1746 to counter the Young Pretender's rebellion. Wander across the Links and under the coast-hugging railway line. (Bridge 67). The sands here once were crowded with holidaymakers. An Edwardian photograph shows police having to do crowd control for a sandcastle competition! Turn left to walk to the end of the promenade. The older building there was once a popular tearoom.

If miles of sand stretch away out to some rocks (the Black Rocks) then make the most of this and rim round the margin of the sea to Pettycur and Kinghorn. Stumps of posts in the sand were wartime defences against any *airborne* landing. Each June there is a popular Black Rock Race from Kinghorn round the skerry and back. The starting time depends on the state of the tide!

If the sea is lapping up to make shore access impossible, go under the railway again (Bridge 69) and turn right along the main road past the Kingswood Hotel, the Alexander III monument and the sprawl of Pettycur Bay caravan park, left. At the Sandhills caravan park, right, take the enclosed footpath down to Pettycur Bay and harbour. If the tide is out or falling the vast Pettycur sands would be the most rewarding

Walking out to the Black Rocks off Burntisland.

choice: miles of pristine sands with Inchkeith anchored out in the estuary and Edinburgh off to starboard.

If having to take the road, the Kingswood Hotel is re-nowned and there is a big restaurant, café, swimming pool and shop complex at the Pettycur Bay Holiday Park, while Kinghorn has cafés on its High Street. The 1887 obelisk to Alexander III, last of the Celtic kings, should not be missed. He rode over the cliffs (grey conglomerates) here one wild night in 1286, bringing to an end a sort of Golden Age and creating one of the great *ifs* of history. If only he had had patience and sired a male heir. If only he hadn't insisted in crossing the Queen's ferry that afternoon, against all advice, if only he hadn't set off in stormy dusk for his castle, and new queen Yolande, at Kinghorn. He was found dead at the foot of the cliffs next morning. His granddaughter and heir, Margaret, the Maid of Norway, died in Orkney on the way back to Scotland, thereby leaving the succession wide open to clamorous claimants. Edward I, asked to arbitrate, said he'd have it himself, which led to the Wars of Independence, Bruce and Bannockburn, the Stuarts (who ironically, became England's monarchs) and all of history since... The night be-fore, at a dinner, the Earl of Dunbar asked the seer of Earlston (True Thomas) if anything noteworthy would happen the next day. He asked in jest but was warned of 'a day of calamity... the worst that Scotland has ever known.'

An alternative or addition which is particularly pleasing early or late is to go up **the Binn**. You can do an hour's round of the Binn or, as described in Appendix I, traverse it and reach Kinghorn cross-country. Either way, start from the end of the esplanade.

As mentioned earlier, if the tide is lapping the rocky railway embankment, you take the alternatives, but try to walk the sands. They are popular with local walkers and sports folk. Note that an 'escape', shown on some maps, does not exist. At nearer full tides too, the last approach to Pettycur is by a rough scrambly path worn below the cliffs—topped by caravans with enviable views. (The decaying volcanic rock makes for many flowers, wild and garden escapes.) This lands you on the small Pettycur Bay. A path leads up by the caravans to reach the A921 coast road. Modern houses now back the bay on what was once a bottleworks site (closed in 1982), and, before that, salt works. The crags above have a prow, Witches' Point, where these unfortunates were burned (the last in 1644), just outside a cemetery. Before the cemetery there was a leech loch which mysteriously drained away, long before the coast road was built in 1842 or the railway cut through Kinghorn. There are a lot of Polish names on the stones, as their forces were based in Fife during the war. Many stones are flat, being blown over by the great gale of February 1968, a gale which blocked every possible route out of Fife as I found out. From the information board by the houses steps lead up to a fine viewpoint.

Pettycur has a single, rather battered 1760 harbour arm with a few boats and huts, contrasting with its history as an important ferry. Storms damaged the original harbour in 1625 and it silted up badly. (There are 17 steps in the corner, for instance—but how many can you count?) A prize of £1000 was offered to solve this problem of silting, and the answer was to build a tidal pool where the car park is now and, at low tide, to let this out in a spate which washed away the accumulated sand. Kinghorn originally was the town up along the High Street and running down to the next bay; Pettycur was the ferry area and, all across Fife, milestones are made out to Pettycur, to the puzzlement of many. Alexander III's castle stood up above the harbour somewhere, on what was Crying-oot Hill. I suspect this was from a message being yelled up to the town pubs to say the next ferry was coming in. Pettycur is one of the *pit-/pet-* prefixes indicating Pictish

origins, and not *petit coeur* as I've heard suggested. Kinghorn
has nothing to do with kings or horns. The first part is *ceann*,
meaning head, *gorn* was a marsh (Kinghorn loch?). A thirteenth century map has it Kyngorn.

   Inchkeith is now at its closest to the Fife shore and, as it is in
Kinghorn parish, I'll describe it here. The island has no tourist
boat running out to it, so a visit would depend on private
arrangements or chartering. The population is mostly gulls
which, scavenging in refuse tips, are often suffering various
fatal epidemics (botulism, etc). There is also a population of
puffins. A good harbour makes landing easy enough, once
there. Weekend yachts are the main visitors today, their
spray-painted graffiti an eyesore. With the mixture of ruins,
jungle and gulls Inchkeith is no beauty spot.

   The king Malcolm II, hard-pressed by Danish attacks,
rewarded the northerner, Robert de Keith, with the island
for his help in fending off the Vikings, and though it didn't
remain long in the Earl Marischal family, the name has stuck.
Through the centuries it has been a fortress of one sort or
another. Since the government sold it off there have been
attempts at having it as an animal sanctuary, a children's
playground or an exclusive Edinburgh commuters' resort.
The next daft idea is about due.

   James IV housed a dumb woman with two children on
Inchkeith to see what, if anything, they would learn to speak.
Both 'languages of God' (Hebrew and Gaelic) were claimed,
but the truth was they didn't speak any language as such.
Mary Queen of Scots visited, of course, and it was held by the
English during her 'Rough Wooing'. James VI destroyed all
defences as a pacifying move. Princess Anne has also been on
Inchkeith; she is Patron of the Northern Lighthouse Board and
has a Munroist's enthusiasm for ticking the list of lighthouses.
Two most unlikely visitors were James Boswell and Dr Johnson.

   Many lighthouse experiments were made on the island,
such as introducing the dioptric system, but in 1899 when
the foghorn was installed it sounded non-stop for 130 hours,
which nearly drove Fife residents crazy. It was then turned
to face out to sea. Today the friendly roar has gone and the
light is automatic. Despite these aids a fisheries cruiser, the
Switha 'took the ground' in 1980 and is still a stark landmark
off the SE corner.

   Inchkeith was the first light built solely by Robert Stevenson
of the famous engineering family, in 1804. The Bell Rock (off

The Lighthouse at Inchkeith.

the Tay, 1811) and the Isle of May (further out in the Forth, 1816) were also his. A Thomas Smith began this four-generation connection with lighthouses. In the late eighteenth century life was precarious, and he lost several children and two wives before finally marrying a lady, herself twice widowed and the mother of Robert Stevenson, who became Smith's partner and successor and married one of Smith's daughters as well. Their sons, Alan, David and Thomas (father of R.L.S.) were all lighthouse engineers, as were David's two sons, one of whose sons only died in 1971. Kirkcaldy, Leven, Anstruther, Crail and St Andrews all have Stevenson harbour works. Thomas Smith made his fortune from lighting the streets of Edinburgh. He fitted out an Elie-built sloop for the Northern Lighthouse Board and the name *Pharos* has been used by service vessels ever since.

Take the road up from Pettycur Harbour whose importance as a ferry lasted till the railway ferry years. The road curves up and, if followed, leads to the High Street. The once-popular novelist Annie S. Swan lived on Pettycur Road. At the top of the road is the war memorial, by Alexander Carrick (he did the Wallace figure at the entrance to Edinburgh Castle). Turn off at a footway with the odd name of Doodells Lane (a corruption of 'two delfs', an old local measure) which leads you round above Kinghorn Bay where the parish church can be seen. At one time there was a shipyard beyond, specialising in ferry boats. In the eighteenth century Kinghorn was bigger than Kirkcaldy

Kinghorn, the old parish church beyond the railway.

and a dozen tall chimneys would be belching out smoke; a very different view now. Quarrel Brae refers to the battle when Macbeth and Banquo defeated a Danish invasion force. During Henry VIII's 'Rough Wooing' and the Battle of Pinkie (1547) the English burnt Kinghorn and killed over 400 people. Cromwell did much the same. Zigzag down to the shore at the RNLI station to walk round to the church.

The path comes out at Harbour Road. Turn down this, but if wanting the town, or the view, the steps opposite go up to Kinghorn station with the town inland of the line. We walk down and then the route turns up under the arches but, before that, turn down to visit the church. The church, though hardly impressive, is quite historic (1774 on a thirteenth-century base) and gives a viewpoint over Kinghorn Bay. If you peer through the nearest window you can see a 1569 ship model hanging in the Sailors' Aisle. One gravestone has the symbol of a plough on it and another relates to a Kirkcaldy tragedy described later: 'Alexander [Dougal], aged 13, who suffered among many others by the fall of a gallary (*sic*) in Kirkcaldy's church, 15th June 1828'. (The Dougal family had already lost two boys, aged one and eight.) One Kinghorn minister's wife, thought to be dead, was buried alive and only recovered when the sexton was struggling to steal the rings from her cold fingers. In a corner is a coffin-shaped mort stone—to defeat grave-robbers. Kinghorn's most forgotten person of note is Christina Robertson (1796–1854), who became a famous portrait painter. She was court painter to Tsar Nicholas I, but

Kinghorn Bay in winter.

died as the Crimea War began and in the following years was simply forgotten.

Head up under the arches of the striding 1846 viaduct (Nethergate). At an extravagant childrens' play area the signposted FCP leads off to head for Kirkcaldy. The path goes under the railway then runs awhile between railway and a caravan park to reach a bay with some curious names. The inlet at the far end is Hoch-ma-toch and the town end is called Bellypuff. The old shipyard was near there. As there was no dock, ships had to be launched completed and with steam up. Engines came by train and the overhead crane transferring them was made from girders retrieved from the Tay Bridge disaster. The yard closed in 1922. They'd built ferries for the Granton-Burntisland run.

The rocks at the far end of the bay are lavas which have flowed from the Binn; you can almost see their movement and expect the sea to hiss with steam. Underneath are the obvious levels of limestone and shale, all displayed for a geology lesson. A well, easily overlooked, descending, once refreshed working horses and drouthy cadgers.

The path zigzags up to gain height, running close by the railway to reach steps up to a wall at the highest point, an extensive viewpoint over the Forth. The FCP runs on through thorn thickets beside the railway and then angles down towards the ruin of Seafield Tower. Below this slope lies the secretive Seafield Cave, a narrow slot running in over 100 feet, redolent of smuggling days and probably the deepest cave on

Heading towards Seafield Tower.

the coast. It was originally longer, but railway construction in 1847 caused a collapse. Low tide gives access. To visit the cave without backtracking from near the castle, turn down the east side of the wall to a rougher path which descends to the bridge that spans the entrance, a bridge renewed in 2003 through the efforts of the Kirkcaldy Civic Society. Beyond are thickets of thorn and the faint remains of limekilns which lead on towards the castle. The rocks offshore often have seals on them and the coast can be lively with migrant wading birds. Just above the tideline before the castle there is a spring which may have served the castle, the seat of the Moultrays. The last of the family perished in the 1715 Jacobite Rising and the castle was abandoned thereafter.

From the castle a gritty road leads on, passing a big harbour arm, built in 1889 but never used thanks to disputes—and who would want a harbour set among all those reefs (a steamship, *Adam Smith*, ran aground on them on Boxing Day 1884), reefs much loved by seals who will be heard 'singing' in season. A ruined brick culvert takes the Tyrie Burn to the sea. The Tyrie bleach-works once employed 70 people who regularly walked there from Kinghorn or Kirkcaldy along what is our coastal path. There was also a 400m. long ropeworks' building further on, a long, long building where the hawsers were twisted together. This scruffy, rocky stretch once had popular sands with Punch and Judy shows, but human alterations led to the sea washing it all away.

The most recent industry to come and go was mining. Where the houses stand up on the left there were once the twin winding towers of the Seafield Colliery (seen in the picture on p.64) which only opened in 1954—and some of us watched the towers toppled by an explosion in 1988. Much of the area has been landscaped, with a parking area and an extensive grassy area above the better sands. Head right of the big grey building at the far end (Morrison's) to gain the Esplanade of **Kirkcaldy** (kir-coddy), made a Royal Burgh in 1450. In the spring the esplanade is given over to the Links Market, now a giant funfair but going back to medieval times. You'll see why Kirkcaldy is called the Lang Toon. But did you know, 'The deil's deid and burried in Kirkcaldy'? One of the many stories concerning Michael Scott ('The Wizard') is a battle he had with the devil who plagued him, nightly, for work, which he always grimly performed and came back for more. Scott finally was rid of him: he told him to come down to the shore here and make a rope of sand, an endless task. Michael Scott was a whizz kid of the thirteenth century, a scholar at Oxford, Paris and Toledo and Professor of Rhetoric at Bologna, philosopher, doctor, Arabic scholar, mathematician and chemist. He was nicknamed The Wizard and incredible stories accrued about him—such as that he cleft the Eildons into three (the Romans called them Trimontium a millennium earlier).

At the start (south end) of the esplanade, overlooking the Tiel Burn, is a big car park with a snack bar and toilets. 'South end' may cause raised eyebrows, and local people too all talk of the east or west end of the High Street or esplanade when the town lies north south due to the curvature of the big bay. It is almost as surprising to discover Kirkcaldy is further west than Carlisle, or Liverpool.

The esplanade should be followed to the first set of traffic lights. Cross there onto Nicol Street. On the right side the garden area has been created in what was the Volunteers Green, a training area for the Napoleonic 'Territorial Army'. Cannons faced out to sea. They might have come in following the raid by John Paul Jones. He anchored offshore and threatened to bombard the town unless paid £200,000, a lot of money in 1778. The Rev. Robert Shirra went down to the Pathhead Sands and led prayers for the town's deliverance. An offshore gale promptly blew the marauder away.

At the next set of traffic lights turn right onto the High Street and through another set to reach the pedestrianised part of the town, very much the centre of Kirkcaldy. Town signs proclaim it the birthplace of Adam Smith.

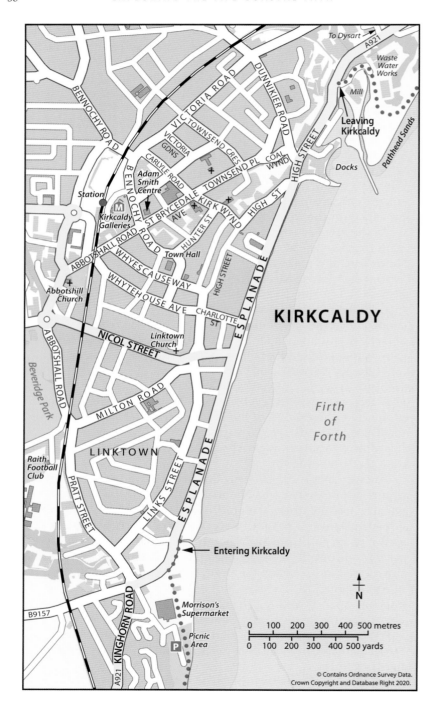

To Dysart
A921

Waste
Water
Works

Mill

Leaving
Kirkcaldy

Pathhead Sands

Docks

BENNOCHY ROAD

VICTORIA ROAD

DUNNIKIER ROAD

TOWNSEND CRES

VICTORIA
GDNS

CARLYLE ROAD

HIGH STREET

COAL
WYND

Adam
Smith
Centre

Station

BENNOCHY ROAD

ST BRYCEDALE AVE

TOWNSEND PL

KIRK WYND

HIGH ST

M

Kirkcaldy
Galleries

HUNTER ST

HIGH ST

ABBOTSHALL ROAD

KIRKCALDY ROAD

Town Hall

WHYESCAUSEWAY

WHYTEHOUSE AVE

HIGH STREET

ESPLANADE

KIRKCALDY

Abbotshill
Church

CHARLOTTE
ST

A ABBOTSHALL ROAD

NICOL STREET

Linktown
Church

Firth
of
Forth

Beveridge Park

MILTON ROAD

LINKTOWN

Raith
Football
Club

PRATT STREET

LINKS STREET

ESPLANADE

Entering Kirkcaldy

B9157

KINGHORN ROAD

A921

Morrison's
Supermarket

P   Picnic
Area

0   100   200   300   400   500 metres
0   100   200   300   400   500 yards

N

© Contains Ordnance Survey Data.
Crown Copyright and Database Right 2020.

A High Street plaque indicates his mother's house where he wrote the seminal *Wealth of Nations*. He was born in Kirkcaldy in 1723. At the age of three he was kidnapped from Strathendry Castle by tinkers. One of the stalwarts of the Scottish enlightenment, he was a friend of people like David Hume and Robert Adam, the latter another Kirkcaldy lad. William Adam (b.1689) was the son of a Kirkcaldy mason who became a big-time entrepreneur in coal, salt, milling, brewing, land and farming besides creating the masterpieces of Haddo, Mellerstain, Hopetoun, House of Dun and Tingwall. Even so he was to be overshadowed by his son Robert, and Robert's three brothers. Robert was born in 1728, but his schooling was disrupted by 'the Forty-five' and he travelled on the continent for some years. By the time he died in 1792, his buildings, monuments and fortifications ranged from Kent to Antrim and Cornwall to Fort George, and his influence remains to this day.

The town's oddest famous literary figure of that period was a girl who died in 1811 at the age of eight. Marjory Fleming's *Diary* has seldom been out of print since. She might have been forgotten had not Dr John Brown (of *Rab and His Friends* etc) romanticised her story, made her a friend of Sir Walter Scott and called her 'Pet' Marjorie as she is described on her portrait memorial in Abbotshall churchyard. My favourite symbol stone in that cemetery is one of crossed rake and spade, indicating a gardener.

One Kirkcaldy sporting hero is now largely forgotten. John Thomson played football for the local coal mine team and was signed up by a scout who'd come to watch the opponent's goalkeeper. He played in several cup-winning teams, but in 1931, playing for Celtic in an Old Firm meeting, he dived at the feet of an attacker and received a kick which proved fatal.

Wheels within wheels: Marshall Keith (a Jacobite exile whose family name

Marjory Fleming's memorial in Abbotshall churchyard.

gives the island off Kirkcaldy its name of Inchkeith) was once involved in peace negotiations with the Turks, in Turkey, on behalf of Russia (with the commissioners and translators all conducting business with great solemnity). Business over, the Turkish vizier then took the Marshall aside and welcomed him in thick Kirkcaldy accents. The vizier's father had been town bellman and he had 'spied they Keiths in the toon whan they wis aw chiels the gither'.

Walking up Whitecauseway from the High Street, one comes to the Town House. Turn right at the crossroads and walk along behind it to see the collection of six decorative old Provost's lamps from the burghs that 'died' in the 1975 changes to local administration: Burntisland, Kirkcaldy, Dysart, Buckhaven and Methil, Leven, Markinch and Leslie. (Leslie had no lamp.) The bus-station is opposite. The Town House was started in 1939 and completed after the war. Wall sculpture and green copper spire are notable and there's a large stair mural. The weathervane on top shows St Bryce.

A plaque in the Town House mentions six famous sons of Kirkcaldy: Robert Adam, Adam Smith, Robert Philp, Dr John Philip, Sandford Fleming and John MacDouall Stuart. Stuart will be mentioned later, Sir Sanford Fleming was an engineer who surveyed the Canadian Pacific Railway and the inventor of world Standard Time, Philp and Philip were related but not happily. Philp was a rich linen-manufacturer and philanthropist who was very annoyed when relatives changed the spelling of the name. 'If ma name isna guid enough for thems, then neither is ma siller.' Doctor John was the first superintendent of the London Missionary Society, and it was to him Doctor David Livingstone reported on his arrival in South Africa.

Head on, inland, from there and cross at the lights ahead. Right lies the Adam Smith Centre (a Carnegie gift), a complex of theatre, halls and café, left is the war memorial garden, always a showpiece (as is the large Beveridge Park, at the west side of the town) overlooked by the Library and award-winning Museum and Art Gallery. Walk through the gardens. The war memorial itself has a horrifying number of names on it (over 1350). John Nairn, of the linoleum family, gifted the integrated site to be the town's memorial. Other art donators were the linoleum manufacturing Blyth family. Michael Portillo's grandparents were related to the Blyths and he spent schoolday holidays in Kirkcaldy. After the big

Kirkcaldy Town House.

commercial attractions like Sea World, the 'Fife Galleries' is Fife's largest tourist attraction, which speaks for itself. The museum is well planned (note a chair made of *coal!*), and there are varying exhibitions in the galleries, besides the more permanent displays, particularly rich in works by William McTaggart, S. J. Peploe and E. A. Hornel. The café is popular too. The most crowd-pulling exhibitions in the last few years were on Peploe and the contemporary Jack Vettriano, originally from Leven. Posters of his strange work outsell Monet or Van Gogh and have made the former miner a millionaire. The stone for the building came from the Grange Quarry on the Binn at Burntisland.

The railway station lies behind the museum, a modern building following a fire caused by vandals. What changes? Burntisland station was burned down by vandals in 1914. On the wall by the station is a Victorian (VR) letterbox. A public outcry saw it put back when an attempt was made to install a replacement. In the station a popular old poem hangs on the wall (inscribed on linoleum) about taking the train to Kirkcaldy. The last couplet goes, 'For I ken mysel' by the queer-like smell / That the next stop's Kirkcaldy!' Linoleum is still manufactured in a small way, so occasionally there is the nice smell of hot linseed oil on the air. A few more comments on people and places as we set off from the town are held for the next section.

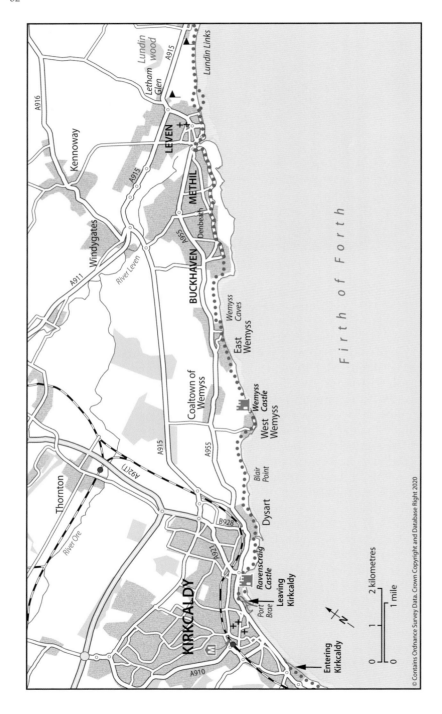

Thornton

River Ore

KIRKCALDY

A910

Entering
Kirkcaldy

Leaving
Kirkcaldy

Port
Brae

Ravenscraig
Castle

A921

B928

Dysart

Blair
Point

A955

A915

West Wemyss

Wemyss
Castle

Coaltown
of Wemyss

A955

A915

East
Wemyss

Wemyss
Caves

BUCKHAVEN

River Leven

Denbeath

A955

A915

METHIL

A915

LEVEN

Letham
Glen

Lundin
wood

A915

Lundin Links

Kennoway

Windygates

A916

A911

A92(T)

A92(T)

Firth of Forth

2 kilometres

1 mile

N

0   1   2

0   1

© Contains Ordnance Survey Data. Crown Copyright and Database Right 2020

IV
The Old Coal Coast
(Kirkcaldy to Leven)

O.S. 59 / 367

This is a ten-mile walk with the last three miles inescapable pavement pounding, but a surprising number of interesting places milestone the route, so there has had to be a selection rather than detailed coverage. Variety is the Spice of Fife. Dysart and Buckhaven offer refreshment stops.

Head along the High Street. Tolbooth Street, right, has no tolbooth now. Kirk Wynd, left, ends the pedestrianised stretch and is one bit of Kirkcaldy with any appearance of antiquity. The Old Kirk (the parish church) was consecrated in 1244 but only the tower dates back to that time. Below it a Victorian house incorporates battlements, turrets, coat-of-arms, the lot, even a dragon on the gully box. Next door is a typical old house with crow-step gables and red pantiles and MA/ML marriage lintel (Matthew Anderson, a corn merchant, and Margaret Livingstone). A plaque (same side, further on) notes 'Thomas Carlyle lodged here 1816–1818. His school is opposite'. This old burgh school has long gone. Another who taught there under Carlyle was Edward Irving, the famous preacher. Their tangled lives almost deserve Big Screen treatment. Irving graduated at 17 and took a teaching post at Haddington. He tutored Jane Welsh, the doctor's daughter, and fell in love with her when she was only thirteen while he was already engaged to the minister's daughter. He introduced Jane to Thomas Carlyle and *they* eventually married; and both have lasting fame. Irving after 12 years grudgingly married his determined fiancée. He became assistant to Thomas Chalmers, one of the ecclesiastical giants of the time, but left for London to become a popular preacher. His excesses led to his being excommunicated, so he formed his own church. He had one last, tragic contact with Kirkcaldy. In 1807 a huge horseshoe gallery had been made out of the old guilds' lofts in the parish church, and when he preached there in 1828 the crowd was so great the north gallery collapsed and 28 people died in the accident or resulting panic. Irving and Carlyle once *rowed* from Kirkcaldy to visit Inchkeith.

Stormy seas at Kirkcaldy: in the distance the towers of the now lost Seafield Colliery.

The church had the spire blown off the tower on Christmas Eve 1900, and in 1968 the galleries were removed and the inside remodelled, only for a vandal's fire in 1986 requiring much new restoration work. (A taxi driver saw smoke coming from the tower in the early hours of the morning and raised the alarm.) The chancel windows are by Burne-Jones, and the contemporary west windows are striking, slender columns of colour and light.

Kirkcaldy only became the major local town with the Industrial Revolution, but a church stood here back in the earliest days. Large populations often meant lively religious life, with churches dominating every aspect of social behaviour. Kirkcaldy threw up many famous ministers, and to this day there are over 40 varied places of worship; beside the large denominations you can find everything from the Apostolic Church to Zionists, via Mormons, Jehovah's Witnesses, Brethren, Quakers, Spiritualists, the Salvation Army and Scotland's only Coptic church. There's also a mosque.

On the High Street (near Kirk Wynd) is a marker for the medieval town cross site. It was demolished in 1782. Where the High Street overtakes the Esplanade there's a fifteenth-century merchant's house (Laws Close) on the left. Continue on the A955 (still High Street) along to the harbour, largely hidden behind flats. Across the street is the Sailors Walk, another fifteenth-century survivor. Charles II (after his Scone Coronation) and Mary Queen of Scots stayed here. The harbour was built for whaling rather than general trade or fishing, and was at its busiest when importing cork for the linoleum manufacturing which dominated inland from the harbour area for a century. In 1644 Kirkcaldy had 100 ships registered, then came the Civil War: 200 local men died at the Battle of Kilsyth in 1645, and five years later 480 died defending the town against Cromwell's troops when 50 ships were lost. A few years later only 12 ships were registered. We forget the past horrors. In 1584 plague killed 300 Kirkcaldy people.

There is quite a *den* inland here, all unnoticed, once the haunt of a young John Buchan whose father was a minister in Pathhead and only left for Glasgow when JB was fourteen. His sister, novelist O. Douglas, was born here. The opening scene of *Prester John* is set on Pathhead Sands and steps down may have inspired the 39. *The Free Fishers* starts with the nail-makers and weavers of Pathhead. The house at the top, Path House, is seventeenth-century and attractive (there's a two-faced sundial) and modern houses have been made to agree with it, unlike the tower blocks beyond.

Near Path House is the Feuars burial-ground (locked because of vandalism) which has a connection with the Porteous Riots in Edinburgh in 1736. Andrew Wilson was a baker in Flesh Wynd and did some smuggling on the side. 'English' taxes on Scotland after the 1707 Union encouraged this. Wilson and a friend, Robertson, robbed a custom's officer at Pittenweem, were caught and condemned to be hanged in Edinburgh. Taken to church for their last service, Wilson seized their guards and yelled at Robertson to run for it. With some help from the congregation he made his escape. Next day Wilson was hanged and the irate mob stoned the guards. Captain Porteous, a weak, lazy bully of a man ordered them to open fire and several people were killed. He was tried in turn, condemned to death, then reprieved, which so enraged public opinion that a mob broke in to his quarters, dragged him off and hanged him from a dyestaff in the Grassmarket.

This end of Kirkcaldy is dominated by the bulk of Carr's Hutchison flour mills. As well as from Fife, grain comes into the harbour from the Continent and Canada. We turn in to walk through the mills—with minimalist FCP signing. The route turns left past the big silos, then heads out alongside the burn towards the Pathhead Sands. Before the dunes our path turns left to the big carparking/recreational area. From

Ravenscraig Castle.

the far end a railed, concrete walkway leads on round the jut of crag with Ravenscraig Castle on it. Pathhead is mentioned in an old jingle:

> Dysart for coal and saut,
> Pathhead for meal and maut,
> Kirkcaldy for lassies braw,
> Kinghorn for breakin the law.

The castle on its prow of red sandstone dominates bays to both sides, and was the romantic setting for Scott's *Lay of the Last Minstrel*. From here the unfortunate Rosabelle set off over the Forth, only to be drowned. Sadly the castle is no longer maintained as its historical position deserves. There is no custodian and some of the best features are locked because, unsurprisingly, vandalism is rife.

Ravenscraig Castle (Historic Scotland) was the first to be built to cope with the new weapon of attack, cannon. In places the walls are 14 feet thick and the slanting roof was designed to deflect cannon balls. Ironically, the castle's creator, James II, was killed by a cannon exploding when he was laying siege to Roxburgh Castle. Ravenscraig was completed by his widow, Mary of Gueldres, but soon passed to the Sinclair family, who owned it till 1896. The castle is worth a look, Hans Christian Anderson thought so. The prow has a small cave at the seaward end, which was once bigger but much of the roof collapsed in 1740, killing ten boys. There's another cave just round the corner, protected by a grille.

The FCP rounds the prow (vivid red sandstone) and skirts the top of the next bay to a flight of steps. At some high tides this may be impossible, in which case backtrack, and head in under the castle to a flight of steps, head to the roundabout and take the A955 to reach Ravenscraig Park.

The steps from the bay lead up to a well-preserved sixteenth-century beehive doocot. If wanting to visit the castle take the steps up and head left, otherwise continue along above the sea through the delightful woods of **Ravenscraig Park**. We won't have woodland walking as good till heading up the River Tay from Balmerino. The sea wall weaves in and out in a rather ridiculous manner, following every indentation of the coast, and was built by the spiteful laird to stop miners walking along the shore to work. The Earl of Rosslyn was so unpopular that the masons came back at night to knock down their own labours. The park was his demesne and linked to Dysart House, his home, by a private bridge. Irony there too, for Rosslyn had to sell everything to pay off enormous gambling debts, and the new owners, the Nairns, gifted the park to the town. The small tower jutting out on the wall is a good spot to watch wintering waders on the rocks below. There's a rock slab inscribed with a poem 'Stanes' by the late Duncan Glen, a Fife-based polymath (*Collected Poems, 1966-2008*).

When a breach in the wall is reached there is the option of going down to the seaside grassy area and round to reach Dysart harbour by a tunnel. Better, continue (keeping by the wall) to a crenellated viewpoint looking straight down into the harbour and away out to North Berwick Law and the Bass Rock or, upriver, to Arthur's Seat. A hundred yards on go through a gap in the wall to a high circuiting path above the harbour. From its end steep steps (or road) descend to the harbour of **Dysart**.

The inner harbour was cut down into solid rock and opened in 1831. Coal was the main export, carted from local mines (a cargo

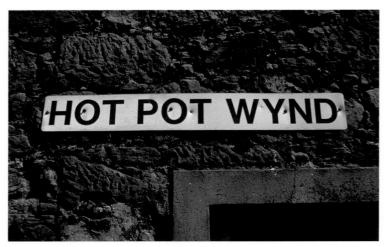

Street sign, Dysart.

was 250 cart-loads). The eighteenth century Harbourmaster's House is now an award-winning interpretive centre, well worth visiting before going on. The Fife Coast and Countryside Trust has its headquarters in the building and there's an excellent café/bistro (tel. 01592 654862). The harbour stood in for Le Havre in *Outlander*.

The road up from the harbour is Hot Pot Wynd, a corruption of the Dutch word for a brae (*het pat*). The Netherlands connection was such that Dysart folk were called Little Hollanders. A Carmelite Monastery now occupies Dysart House (up Hot Pot Wynd). The area beyond the harbour is tidied up with grass and car parks, but once was a major site for salt production, a dirty, laborious business: it took 32 tons of sea water and 16 tons of coal to produce one ton of salt. Water was pumped from the sea into huge pans and boiled over coal fires till the water evaporated. Pan Ha' is from Pan Haugh, the level ground where the pans operated. The Fife coast was a major salt-producer because coal was so readily available. Salt and coal, beer and fish all went to the Low Countries and the return imports included cartwheels, Delftware, kegs of Hollands, pipes of Rhenish and the familiar pantiles. There was much trade with Scandinavia and Germany too. Scotland has always been European in a way England never was.

Coal made Dysart a prosperous town, but at a price. There were awful accidents. In 1476 the town nearly vanished in an explosion; there was another in 1578 and multiple deaths in 1662, 1700, 1791… By 1912 over 900 miners were employed in the Lady Blanche, the Frances (Sinclair names) and Randolph (a Wemyss name). A tunnel brought coal from the first right to the port and also acted as a ventilation shaft, as did an older stair pit, the Violet. A 'stair pit' was just that; after the coal was 'putted' (pulled) to the foot of the shaft it was carried up on the backs of women and children, who worked 12 hours a day. Miners were no better than serfs until 1799, when some alleviating legislation began.

The castle-like tower is of St Serf's church, little of which remains. The north aisle was removed to make the road down to the harbour. Before the Reformation the local priest Walter Myln was arrested and burnt at the stake in St Andrews for heresy. In 1642 a Margaret Young was imprisoned in the tower for ten weeks on a charge of witchcraft. That was a nasty century. Town minutes of 1633 record monies paid out for dealing with two witches: 'For 10 loads of coal to burn them, For a tar barrell, For towes, To the executioner, To him that brought the executioner, For the executioner's expenses, £14. 4s. 6d'. In 1649 the Dysart minister, an 'expert', was called to Burntisland to test a witch by sticking a pin into her flesh, and the result was proof of guilt, so she was burned the same day.

Walk along the attractive row of red-roofed, white harled houses, restored in the 1960s under the National Trust for

Pan Ha', Dysart.

Scotland's 'Little Houses Scheme', which saved many small dwellings on the Fife coast. The first building was once the Bay Horse Inn. There's a dated lintel (1583) round the back, part of the old manse, inscribed, 'My hoip is in the Lord'. The reef offshore is the Partan Craig, 'partan' being the edible crab. Alleys leading up from the houses are Saut Girnal Wynd (salt store lane) and Hie Gate (high lane). Go up the latter (FCP sign), climbing past the 1582 house, the Anchorage. Once up, head for Rectory Lane but pass right of the white corner house with the commemorative plaque. This is to John Mac-Douall Stuart, the first person to have crossed Australia south to north in 1861-62. Born in Dysart in 1815, he emigrated in 1839. He was on Captain Sturt's expedition five years later, then mounted expeditions of his own to Lake Eyre and the centre of Australia. Two previous attempts on the complete south-north had failed, so his ultimate 2000-mile journey was quite a feat. He returned by the same route.

Continue to reach the High Street. Note the long pavement inscription. Turn right to the attractive old tolbooth with an outside stair and the date 1576, when it was probably first erected. The Town House stair (next door, 1617) shows a simplified version of the town's crest, a bare tree with exposed roots. In 1840 there was a report of the prison in the tolbooth being 'quite unsuitable… dry, but not very secure'. Cromwell stored gunpowder in the tower and an accident 'blowed off the roofe… so scarcely remained a sclait'. We continue straight on but, if enthusiastic for Fife's old buildings, turn left up Cross Street to Quality Street to see a superbly restored building, The Towers, dated 1586. The house next door has a 1610 marriage lintel. Writers John Buchan and his sister Annie spent a summer holiday in Dysart. One highlight was finding a broody hen on a clutch of eggs—under a bed.

Heading on from the town centre, the High Street eventually becomes Edington Place. A pub, The Man in the Rock, is passed. When the road turns left (at a housing scheme) bear off right. There's a monument for the Frances colliery (in 1959 employing 1,400 miners) and the Fife Coastal Path heads along to pass the Frances colliery site, the winding headgear and settling ponds the only visible evidence now. Both the Frances here and the Michael (ahead) were finally worked from the Seafield at Kirkcaldy. All have gone, virtually without trace. The grassy area to the right of the path disguises the waste tip, the redd being simply dumped into the sea, which is still eroding this coast. The Dubbie Braes, as this area was called before the Frances opened, was a popular Victorian spot with picnics and preachings, political meetings, cricket, dancing and hiking all popular. There was a bandstand. The Volunteers practised firing at a target offshore. Everything was tidied up for Victoria's Jubilee (public wash-house removed etc) when there was an all day (and night) party. The Frances destroyed all that—and now it too has gone.

Follow the fence line on round past the back of an industrial estate, in from Blair Point. There's a brief view of open sea before steps plunge the path down to shore level again, with a sweep of bay leading to pretty West Wemyss. Under Blair Point the 'Red Rocks' (where witches were burnt) have crumbled into the sea, in 1971 taking with them a weaver's 1851 carving illustrating Byron's *Prisoner of Chillon*, known as *The Man in the Rock*. The one-time shore path round west to Dysart has gone.

The bay ahead is shingly, though at one time sandy. Mining subsidence caused the sand to be washed away. The bay is backed by Chapel Wood; any water running out is rusty red, probably from old mineworkings with which the area is riddled. Flints found on the shore came from ballast tipped out at West Wemyss harbour. Our path joins a rough drive with an old tower half-hidden behind a wall with small towers and grilled arches, the work of Robert Lorimer, everything creepy

Heron on the seafront, West Wemyss.

with trees. Hitchcock could have made use of the location, which is actually the burial ground of the Wemyss family. The first chapel may be fifteenth-century, built by Spaniards fleeing the Inquisition. The chapel was destroyed at the Reformation, but in 1627 Lord Elcho (later second Earl of Wemyss) turned it into a house. The First World War Admiral of the Fleet and First Sea Lord, Lord Wemyss is probably the most notable person buried here. We pass certain artworks and the boat club to reach the harbour.

The harbour of **West Wemyss** dates back to the early sixteenth century at least. (In 1590 a barque from plague-infected England put in and passed on the dreaded epidemic.) The white building (Shorehead House, sixteenth-century) has a Dutch gable and is the one-time pilot's house, always painted white to act as a seamark. The harbour has been largely filled in and landscaped. The Victoria pit was sited here, but ran out of coal in 1914. East of Shorehead House the bricked-up arches were the site of the pit pony stables. Another bricked-up arch is a tunnel which went up to the Hugo Mine at Coaltown of Wemyss, which then was linked to Methil docks by rail. The tunnel kept the mining activities decently out of sight of Wemyss Castle. It was bricked up after some school kids became lost in it and nearly died. The building above the houses as we walk on was the Miners' Institute; built in 1927, closed in 1952 and converted into a hotel in 1979 (now closed again).

East, West and Coaltown of Wemyss were built as mining villages. Sadly, with the failure of mining, West Wemyss slipped into decay, its architectural worth ignored. The Coxstool buildings looking onto the harbour offer a fine example of restoration work, however. Coal was exported largely to Middlesborough, Amsterdam and Hamburg. In 1901 West Wemyss had a population of 1,300; in 1981 it was 379. Methil Docks, opened in 1887 to serve steamships, also contributed to the decline of the smaller, older ports. Head off along Main Street, which has been attractively restored.

Dutch influence is seen in the slender tower of the tolbooth with its swan weathervane (the oft-repeated logo of the Wemyss family) and a corner cut away and with a 'pal stone' at its foot to protect the corner from damage by passing wheels. The pend (passage) leads through to what was Duke Street, a corruption of *joug*, meaning jail. The street has been used as a location for a TV serial. I like the name Happies Close (right) near the end of Main Street. The war memorial occupies an old entrance to the churchyard and there's a turning area for vehicles beside the present entrance. Before looking into the kirkyard turn up to the sea wall to see a monument to some 1941 local heroes—in the shape of a mine.

St Adrian's is built of red sandstone with a bold, round west window. Adrian was an early Christian missionary who may have come from Hungary originally. He founded a chapel on the Isle of May but was killed by a Viking raid c. 850. On going in one sees some pathetic marble monuments to children and, past the door, left, to 'sons John, Alex and James who fell in action in France. 1915. 1916. 1917'. Behind the church is a stone with the crown of a hammerman. Against the back wall a big 4 indicates a merchant. And there's a stone with the date of death as 31st April 1878! Inside the church is a gravestone made of coal.

Walking on, the view is dominated by Wemyss Castle, from here a rather bleak-looking pile. A walled-up cave in the first crag is known as Green Jean's Cave after the ghost who appears when there is a death in the castle. (She appeared rather often when the castle was a wartime hospital.) It was at Wemyss Castle Mary Queen of Scots first met Lord Darnley—with all that followed.

We are briefly diverted onto the shore itself. Both shoreline and FCP are taking a hammering from the sea. You could have trouble passing. On a bit, a golf course was opened here in 1850 but abandoned before the end of the century. The Michael colliery (1898-1967) too has gone and improved paths and tree plantings hide all these considerable past activities. At a more open area a FCP sign may point left (across a meadow of blue lupins in summer) for a deviation caused by a factory ahead. As the factory has been demolished, just keep straight on to reach the

Memorial to the Michael Colliery disaster.

East Wemyss War Memorial.

wide grassy frontage of **East Wemyss**.

Below this path there used to be the Glass Cave; the name dating to seventeenth-century glassmaking. In 1901 the cave collapsed due to the workings of the Michael and was filled with *redd* (pit waste). In 1929 ground below a boiler in the pit cracked and a new cave was discovered below. (A piece of graffiti was dated 1690!) Archaeologists were given a grudged period to investigate before the cave was filled with concrete. A cup and ring mark and a hunting scene with an elk was noted; elk, extinct before the time of Christ, gives rise to some interesting speculation about dating the artwork. The Michael closed in 1967 after a disastrous fire that cost nine lives.

Do note the extensive sea defences again. The stone came from Cruicks Quarry which we passed at Inverkeithing and was brought to the site by barges, at high tide. Their bottoms then opened to deposit the stone which JCBs could then work on at low tide. Imagine if all that stone was moved by lorries! The Dysart-Wemyss villages' defences cost £5 million.

Walk along the seafront but follow the road round when it swings left to find Sir Jimmy Shand Court and School Wynd, this starting at the far left corner. Walk up it for a couple of minutes to come on a striking wall mosaic commemorating a 1909 tragedy. The wall blocks off a toilet which was the scene of a particularly vile murder—a story we will follow.

Return to Sir Jimmy Shand Court. On its edge, facing the war memorial, is a bench with the reminder 'Lest we forget'. The war memorial is set in what were the original gates of the earlier parish kirkyard and has a tiny figure of a soldier on top. St Mary's-by-the-sea is on a site dating back to the twelfth century and closed in 1976. The building is now a private house. Most of the stones have weathered badly, but one, 1646, is very early, a 1761 stone has all the Ns incised in mirror image while many fisher feuars from Buckhaven have anchors portrayed. There's also a clear gun and powderhorn (hammerman) stone and one with a plough, which also has graceful calligraphy. The kirkyard can only be visited by prior arrangement with Fife Council (tel. 01592 260277).

Heading seaward, there's a cairn up on the right, a memorial to Jimmy Shand, the world-renowned musician and accordion player. He was born in East Wemyss in 1908, started life in the pits aged 14 and would be knighted in 1999, dying a year later. He lived in Auchtermuchty where there is a statue of him, in kilt, playing his accordion.

Walk past houses to find East Brae which winds up steeply by a chunky building which was once a famous brewery. Go up the brae and in to the huge cemetery by a gate on the right. There is a Rennie Mackintosh designed memorial of no great quality, but it is the dangers of mining and sea—and war—that cry out from the stones. A white cherub marks the grave of 15-year-old Michael (Mickey) Brown, who was 'done to death' in 1909. He had been sent to Buckhaven by tram for the wages of the linen factory (Johnstons', opened 1860 and only closed in 2003) which was situated on the shore. Returning, he was waylaid and murdered by Alexander Edminstone, an unemployed miner, in the School Wynd lavatory mentioned earlier. Edminstone disappeared with the money. There was a tremendous hue and cry and, through a poster in Manchester, he was apprehended and brought back to Fife, crowds greeting his arrival and the press avidly printing his mother's letters to him in Perth prison where he was executed, the last prisoner to be hanged in that place. Mickey's parents had already lost a son, aged two, and a daughter, aged eight months. One brother

The grave of Michael Brown, murdered at the age of fifteen.

'Thor and the Sacred Goat' in the Court Cave.

did live till 1949. His mother died aged 92 in 1952. A booklet tells the horrific story fully: D.J. Currie: *Dark Skies Over School Wynd* (1998).

Return to the East Brae and down to the foreshore. A century ago this beach had sands, but now suffers serious erosion. Many miners built and raced small boats but fishing was never possible. The seas offshore often have ships at anchor and parked oil rigs.

Turning along on our eastward way we come to a set of boards explaining the **Wemyss Caves** which lie ahead. (The boards are on setts in a pattern of the 'dumbbell' symbol, as seen in Jonathan's Cave.) The caves only came to public knowledge in 1865 when symbols matching those of better known Pictish stones were recognised. Recent decades have seen a great deal of storm damage with a lot of erosion threatening the caves. Pictures of *c.* 1850 show a doocot which would now be 80 yards out in the sea. Human vandalism and neglect is a sadder element in much being lost. The inner doo cave collapsed when guns, sited above, were fired in World War I, though this may be a blessing yet with symbols of the swimming elephant (a Pictish beast), Z-rod and so on preserved undamaged on the walls. The caves at present are *very* dangerous and are best appreciated from one of the guidebooks available. They contain more prehistoric cave art than the rest of the country combined. There's a Wemyss

Caves Museum and Visitor Centre at the Terras Hall on The Haugh (continuation off Main Street). Open in summer. Virtual tours: *www.wemysscaves.org*.

The Court Cave comes first, so named as baronial courts may have been held there. Pillars erected in the 1930s failed to stop a major roof collapse in 1970. Cup marks predate the Picts even. One drawing is popularly called Thor and the Sacred Goat. Doo Cave is next, recognisable from the surviving nest boxes now low on the wall. There's an inner cave, as mentioned, and mud flowing from it is building up to obscure some of the nest boxes. A 1945 storm took away the brick wall across the cave mouth which is the safest to enter. Fleeing after the Battle of Culloden, the Chevalier Johnston spent time hiding in the caves.

Beyond the Doo Cave the FCP climbs very steeply up the bank to run along between a cemetery and the remains of Macduff Castle, then joins a gritty track onwards for Buckhaven. By the castle is a picnic table and a path/steps drop down to the shore to access the remaining caves. (The sea has demolished a low-level approach.) The murderer of Mickey Brown hid the leather wages bag at the castle. Macduff's Castle has little interest beyond a stairway down to a cellar, lit by a gun loop. The exterior stonework is honeycombed by weathering. Old pictures show two towers, but the council blew one up in 1967 'for safety'. The castle is connected with

The remains of Macduff Castle, caves below.

the Thane of Fife who slew Macbeth. He had escaped along the coast to cross the ferry to North Berwick and refuge in England, but a castle then would have been constructed of wood. Edward I had a later castle burnt. The Wemyss family bought the castle back into the family in 1630 but let it go to ruin as they resided in Wemyss Castle. The plant Alexanders grows here, as at many castles; it was a sort of medieval celery.

The steps from the castle lead to a grassy bay with Macduff's Castle above—and several caves below, including the once-famous Well Cave where Celtic Samhain (Hallowe'en) festivities gave way to Hansel Monday torchlight processions. Rockfalls make access both dangerous and irresponsible. A passage supposedly led up to the castle.

Continuing, you come to the best of the caves, Jonathan's, said to be named from a one-time resident nailmaker. In 1988 the sea cut back to threaten the cave which is safe enough to enter. All but one of the carvings are on the west wall, the one being far back on the east side and showing the earliest delineation of a ship in Scotland. A graceful swan has given speculation that the Wemyss symbol as well as the Wemyss name (Gaelic for cave) came from here. A boar, fish, bull and various symbols are made out. In 1991 the Royal Museum took casts of everything possible.

Just round the next corner is Sloping Cave but it will only be reached with difficulty and then one will have to come back the same way. Sloping Cave is now easier to enter due to the erosion. There is one carved symbol (left) and several holdfasts for tethering animals. The cave goes in far enough really to need a torch, and blocks on the floor give warning of the unstable roof. Other caves lie further along but are not worth visiting at present. White Cave is a bit of a mystery too. A small hole may be a way in, but excavation would be needed to investigate properly. Myth blows it up to huge dimensions (a passage to Kennoway!). Masonry on the shore is from old gas works, and Gasworks Cave is the last. A 1959 rockfall litters the interior where there was a prehistoric quern. Holdfasts line the east wall. Professor Simpson (of chloroform fame) and Dewar (thermos flask inventor) made the first exploration. Walking back past Jonathan's Cave, head up a grassy track inland which climbs steeply, then crosses fields to reach the gritty grey track mentioned earlier. Turn right; soon the track ends and the continuation, all the way to **Buckhaven**, is a red, gritty path which follows the one-time tramway.

Where the view opens out the slopes below have had several bad landslips in the past, gaps opening large enough to swallow a tractor. Natural regeneration and planting is changing the slopes today and you can walk along the grass parallel to the gritty path (orchids in summer). You eventually have to rejoin the path but, after steps, leave it to walk along the grassy slopes of Viewforth. Well named, the views are now vast and well described on boards—as is everything in and about Buckhaven. Up the Forth the point of West Wemyss (and castle) is clear and, beyond, the point at Kinghorn. The many huts are on the site of a once busy harbour, with 198 boats seeking the 'silver darlings'—the second largest fleet in Scotland.

Buckhaven is the anglicised name for what the locals still call Buckhynd, a *hynd* being a harbour arm, *buc* meaning to roar (both Norse words) and early maps sometimes had it as Hynde of Buck. The harbour has gone and so have the sands that brought *pierrot* shows, bandstands and Punch and Judy entertainment to Victorian children. Daniel Defoe came spying in 1700 and called the place 'miserable', but he had been ripped-off and was unforgiving. A possible tradition is that shipwrecked Dutchmen largely founded the town. Certainly its long history as a fishing port made it a place apart. An 1866 directory lists 100 boats, but only 12 family names among the owners. Weaving was also important, but inter-marrying between the industries was rare for practical reasons really: a weaver lass wouldn't be very good at baiting a long line! A local mill supplied the yarn for the first transatlantic cable.

Walk along to the end of Viewforth and turn left into Randolph Street. Much of Buckhaven was cleared in the sixties, with some hideous flat-roofed boxes erected. Modern developments are more attractive. The big frontage is the old Co-op building, and on the corner when the main road is reached stand the Parish church (St David's) and the one-time Royal Bank of Scotland, the one where the hapless boy Brown drew the wages that led to his being murdered. The former church, St Andrew's (next to St David's) once stood in St Andrews (North Street), but was bought at a knock-down price and shipped, stone by stone, round Fife Ness to Buckhynd in 1872. It is now a theatre. On the right is the Braehead Garden, on the site of the 1960s pioneering Braehead School (closed 1971) where I led expeditions at home and abroad. We completed a school round of the Munros. Our shopping was done at the Co-op; a list could start '3 doz tins sardines, 3kg block cheddar, 40 loaves...'

We walk on, for an hour or two of urban landscape which can't be avoided but is not devoid of interest. Facing the gardens, Stuarts, the bakers/café (prize-winning Scotch pies!) may be welcomed, then, on the right, the library houses an interesting small museum upstairs, open during library hours. On the left the Primary School still occupies an attractive 1915 building. Seawards from here, Rising Sun Road, you can see the huge mast and 'windmill' of the Energy Park, on what was an oilrig construction yard and, until 1967, the site of Wellesley Colliery. Its huge sprawl of *redd* actually buried the hamlet of Links of Buckhaven and spilt into the sea. We still see black tidelines after storms.

At the roundabout turn right along Wellesley Road. This is now Denbeath, though there is no break between Buckhaven and Leven. Wellesley is from another Wemyss family member, wife of Randolph. A certain paternalistic philanthropy went with their exploitation of the populace, and the still attractive hospital building is a high mark. Note the Wemyss swan on a gable wall plaque. The clock hands represent a miner's pick and shovel and the clock chimes each quarter.

When Wellesley Road bends we are right above Energy Park, which is developing the old rig construction yard (and land at the harbour) for a variety of energy projects. Huge sheds and tall floodlighting towers still stand. Much more to come. Heading on, the next interest is on the landward side: a row of houses in the Wemyss style with red roofs and outside stairs. (Several similar rows lie behind.) The White Swan Hotel is a listed building marking the change from Denbeath, a 'new town' before its time, and Methil. On the pavement is an Edward VIII postbox (the only other two known are in Tobermory on Mull). Walk on to reach the small Memorial Park and skirt its seaward edge then to drop down into **Lower Methil**. The local war memorial has the figure of a kilted soldier, and lists 337 names. Ex-servicemen raised funds to stock the library opposite, opened in 1935. The trees were planted by all the local schools to celebrate the 1937 Coronation of George VI. Follow a gritty path to come out on Methil Brae. Turn right, then left onto the High Street.

The building on the corner (red sandstone) has a weathervane of a horse. The brae here was once a mine tramway (as at Dalgety Bay). Methil was linked to Thornton by railway

Weather vane, Lower Methil.

from 1887 till 1966 and there was also a Wemyss Private Railway, and the tramcars. Tracks, stations and the score of mines they served have all disappeared now.

The High Street of Lower Methil is 'penny plain' but you can amuse yourself by looking at house names to find the most pretentious. St Andrew's Square, set back on the right, is an attractive 1930s development which replaced slum housing. Further on, right, the old post office building (red sandstone again) houses the interesting Methil Heritage Centre; worth a visit and maybe a cup of tea. A plaque on the wall has a rare monogram—of Edward VIII. The road comes to a junction; turn left, on Dubbieside, to pass an entrance to an industrial estate and the Bayview home of East Fife Football Club. We reach **Leven** over the Bawbee Bridge. A bawbee is an old Scots halfpenny, which was the toll for the early nineteenth-century suspension bridge which the present bridge replaced, costing £200,000 in 1957, the biggest bridge project since the war.

Seaward from the bridge was a dominant power station which was specially built in the 1960s to gobble up the slurry, waste still being produced from active pits. Now the mining has gone and so have all the bings and waste across the county (which looks so green and tidy as a result). With the disappearance of Edinburgh's sludge boat *Gardyloo* it was perhaps hoped to use that waste! The site was chosen because a plentiful supply of water is needed. The outflow water was warm and in winter appreciative swans and ducks gathered by the score. The site was 'mothballed' then demolished.

The view is now dominated by the Levenmouth Pool and Leisure Centre. Leven had an active harbour at one time, all under the bus station or swimming pool complex area. Coal, linen, whisky, iron, potatoes and bone dust were the main exports. Methil Docks basically killed off Leven as a harbour. A steamer connected Largo, Leven, Dysart with Newhaven across the Forth. In 1828 the River Leven had *c.* 30 mills on it, for spinning, lint, snuff, paper, timber, corn and barley. There were many bleach fields.

A pedestrian crossing leads to the bus station and pedestrianised High Street, the main shopping centre for the urban miles we've walked. Leven will mark a break on our route. Most B&Bs are on the promenade.

One or two things to see. Head along the Promenade and turn left into Seagate, to see two remnants of a one time extensive use of shells, coloured glass, bits of broken pottery etc., in decorating houses and gardens. Return to walk along the car parking area past the attractive two-toned 1874 Grey People's Institute building. The name is from the original benefactor. The building and cottages along Viewforth beyond have the typical Fife 'rusticated quoins'—alternating long and short dressed stones at corners and around the windows, often in contrasting colours or the darker being

Rusticated quoins in Leven.

Beehive symbol on the old Co-op building, Leven.

the local whin stone. Turn left up School Lane, and on to the end of the pedestrianised High Street (the main shopping/eating options are here if wanted). Up on the brick building of the 1887 Co-op building there is a plaque showing a skep with bees flying about. Along, right, a 1935 version by the clock forgot to add the bees!

84

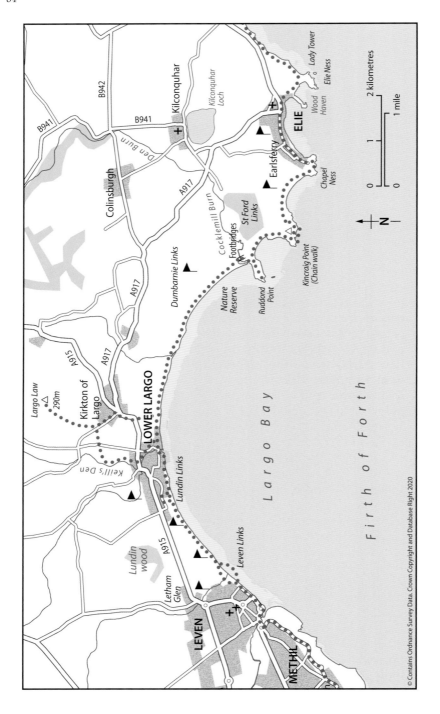

© Contains Ordnance Survey Data. Crown Copyright and Database Right 2020

V
Largo Bay (Leven to Elie)

O.S. 59 / 370, 371

This chapter covers the most rural section of the estuary part of the walk, then comes the interest of the East Neuk towns and, to end, quite the hardest and longest empty miles along what is often, rightly, called the 'Cold Coast'. Today's walking is easy, but it is worth carrying supplies, especially liquid; there are not many watering holes on the eight miles round **Largo Bay**.

The walk is most easily picked up again on the Leven promenade. Heading east again there is a path along by the shore, or you can stay on the road for a while. Note the Festival garden on the left with two monuments commemorating the Polish Parachute Brigade who were based and trained locally during the last war. There's also a curious sundial where you become the gnomon. The end building, in bold red brick, 1894 on gully boxes, a crest on the gable and a text 'What holes wins' points to the 1820 founding of the Leven Golfing Society. The East Neuk is a breeding ground of golf courses. Inland, beyond the bowling green, is the Leven Thistle Golf Club, with whom the links are shared. Inland again is the municipal Scoonie golf course, and, marching eastwards, Lundin golf course (designed by James Braid). The road leads to the Leven Beach Holiday Park (public café/bistro). The site can be passed on the landward side if the preferred beach walk is frustrated by a high tide.

Not far along there is a burn, the boundary between the Leven and Lundin courses. Once a year a golf match between the two is held over half of each course, out and back, with a good social interval in the appropriate clubhouse at the halfway stage. The boundary is more precisely the Mile Dyke, and if this is followed inland, a five minute walk, **Silverburn Park** is reached, a one-time estate now operated by the charity FEAT, based in Glenrothes. There's a beautiful walled garden, marked woodland walks (giant redwoods), tea room in what was once a flax mill, allotments, volunteer garden, camping site and hut accommodation. A lively place and well worth a diversion. An amalgamation of estates took the name Silverburn in 1854 when David Russell established a flax industry, long gone, and planted many exotic trees, now magnificent in their maturity. Return by the Mile Dyke (the iron steps are a viewing point for golfers) and continue on round the bay, the view now dominated by Largo Law.

This could be climbed from Lower Largo (see Appendix 2). The hill (*law* is a common Scots word for hill) is the local weatherman: 'When Largo Law puts on its cowl/ Look out for wind and weather foul'. The coast is more windy than wet—another good reason for walking the Fife coast.

Sands (or dunes at high tide) give a good view round Largo Bay to Ruddons Point. At a burn there is an alternative inland route (only for exceptional high tides) which crosses the golf course and follows roads round its edge (there are many signs). Pass the clubhouse and 120 yards beyond the carpark, at a sign, drop down to the shore level again. The better shore route keeps below the clubhouse, leaves the sands, wends through dunes and joins a track between houses to reach a road running down into Lower Largo.

Follow this road to reach the old harbour/small estuary of **Lower Largo** dominated by the defunct viaduct of the Fife Coast railway, one of Beeching's closures in the sixties. The Railway Inn, a shop and Crusoe Hotel cluster round the mouth of the Keil Burn and can offer refreshments. Walk the twisting Main Street through the long village. An interesting sculpture is passed, the work of Martin Rayner, once sculptor in residence at Kirkcaldy's art gallery (which has two of his works). The Orra (a gap to seaward) is passed and then the

The Tree Avenue, Silverburn.

Lower Largo.

road up to the A915. Then comes the famous statue, wrongly signed as being Robinson Crusoe.

The figure is Alexander Selkirk, the prototype for Defoe's fictional character. Selkirk was born here in 1676 (in an earlier house) and was a bit of a wild lad who eventually went off to sea. He must have been a capable seaman for he was sailing-master of the ill-fated *Cinque Ports*, a ship where captain and crew (particularly Selkirk) were at daggers drawn. Selkirk asked to be put ashore on Juan Fernandez Island, off the South American Pacific coast, rather than continue on what he considered a leaky death trap. He took only a few supplies, for it was an island used for watering ships. He was there for over four years. The *Cinque Ports* sank soon after leaving him, the few captured survivors spending longer years in a Chilean gaol than Selkirk did on his island.

When the road makes the right-angled turn seawards, take the footpath which goes straight on through to a car park, the site of an old drying green. (The house making this road diversion was once a net factory.) There are toilets and

*The statue of Alexander Selkirk
in Lower Largo.*

information boards and, at the landward side, steps go up
to the official coastal path which takes the dull, easy option
of the old railway track. This is only worth following at the
highest of tides, hidden behind the dunes as it runs, and
halfway along the bay it comes down to the shore again anyway. More interest will be found walking on through the last
stretch of Lower Largo, where the road is often banded with
wind-blown sand. This area is Temple, possibly a reference
back to the Knights Templar.

A small tarred road going off up left indicates the Serpentine
Walk to Upper Largo, which is the route to follow if aiming to
climb Largo Law (see Appendix 2). At the final turning spot
of the road there are steps up onto the old railway line too,
but it is more satisfying to wander the extensive sands if the
tide allows. Paths wander along the dunes as well. A stretch
of dunes in the middle of the bay is the SWT Dumbarnie
Links Wildlife Reserve. Oil rigs are often anchored offshore.

Skylarks may be reeling overhead and there's a spacious-
ness unusual on the coast. The estuary has widened too, with
the Lammermuirs rather than Edinburgh's Pentlands across
its waters. Eider, scoter and long-tailed ducks may be seen.
Land snail shells (often at thrushes' 'anvils') are colourfully

banded. Old wartime defences and anti-tank blocks are slowly being swallowed by the dunes and there are plenty of rabbit burrows. Inland lies another golf course. The bay ends at the Cocklemill Burn and Ruddons Point.

The salt marsh here has a summer spread of sea aster. One of the interests of the Fife coast is the huge range of shrubs and flowers to be found along the way. Among those found in wetter parts, see if you can spot kingcups, scurvy grass, butter-bur, forget-me-not, woundwort, primrose, marsh lousewort, yellow flag (iris), dog's mercury, balsam, ragged robin, marsh cinquefoil, knotgrass, meadowsweet, marsh pennywort, sea mayweed, purging flax, sea milkwort, amphibious bistort, marsh felwort, sea spurrey, wormwood, water dropwort, golden saxifrage, watercress, bogbean, various orache, thistle, chickweed, willowherb, dock, sundew, orchids and violet species, quite apart from grasses, reeds and rushes and what flourishes *in* water, salt, brackish or fresh. Oddly, right next to these areas, rocky places can be bright with plants demanding drier quarters: thrift, tormentil, wild strawberry, kidney vetch, coltsfoot, thyme, bedstraw, stonecrops, Scots bluebell, eyebright, valerian, ivy, travellers' joy, gorse, silverweed, sea plantain, burnet rose, restharrow, rock rose, cowslip, poppy and the like. Some areas seem to welcome the barbed wire brigade of blackthorn, brambles, sweetbriar (and nettles) while the grassier slopes can be

In Dumbarnie Links Nature Reserve, Largo Bay.

*Cowslips among the many wild flowers to be seen in
the East Neuk.*

colourful with campions, knapweeds, ox-eyed daisy, yellow
bedstraw, yarrow, scabious, agrimony, cranesbills, comfrey,
ragwort, bindweed, hawkbits, Alexanders and various um-
bellifers. There's also yellow rattle, viper's bugloss, hawkbits,
buttercups, celandine, daisy and dandelion, bracken in some
places, elder and various garden escapes. Both primrose and
wild hyacinth (the English bluebell) seem to cross habitat
boundaries at will, but I've seen snowdrops at the Cambo
Burn in flower *below* the level of a seaweed tidemark!

The **Cocklemill Burn** used to be quite a problem, but a millennium present was its bridging, though there may be times
when you'll paddle along the bridge, judging by seaweed and
plastic junk caught on the structure. There are two sturdy
bridges, in fact, leading up to a wood strip behind which is the
Elie Holiday Park. The café welcomes walkers and camping
is possible. The site can be walked round, or maybe head out
to Ruddons Point (SSSI) first. The Point seems to point at the
windmill in Buckhaven and there's quite a shock at seeing
the scale of the bay we have walked.

I cast my line in Largo Bay
    And fishes catch'd nine.
There were three to boil and three to fry,
    And three to bait the line.

> O, weel may the boatie row,
>   And better may she speed,
> And lees me on the boatie row,
>   That wins the bairnie's bread.
>   Anon.

At the start of last century a couple out walking discovered a prehistoric 'midden', with items like decorated combs, a bone pin, a spindle whorl, a bone cup and remains of ox, sheep, pig, rabbit, red and roe deer, dog and fox and also stones, which were heated and dropped into water to cook food.

Across Shell Bay, running out to the point, the distinctive steps of 'raised beaches' will be observed. (A periodic feature of the East Neuk to look out for.) These indicate former sea-levels and tie in with the various ice ages. From the caravan park, or shore, a burn is crossed and then a path runs between fields of rich soil and the shore.

Turning the point the path climbs the successive levels of the raised beaches. For the second it breaks into steps and, about 50 yards before the last lot of steps, a barely noticed path breaks off, right, very steeply down to shore level. This is the way to the Chain Walk, Scotland's unique *via ferrata*, which is described in Appendix 3. Don't investigate; read the appendix. Easier walking leads to the top of **Kincraig Hill**, 63m., another viewpoint out of all proportion for its modest height. We look back as far as Kinghorn and out in the expanding estuary to the Isle of May. There are several wartime remains and an observation post down some steps. Below on the shore are some strangely flat areas and ruler-straight dykes. There are two communication masts on top. (The trig point is not quite on the highest spot.) A path leads us on, past an obvious gun emplacement, then angles down to **Earlsferry** links and **Elie** golf course. An information board describes the military story. For safety it is better to walk along the sands, themselves attractively warm in colour, and the rocks with beards of green weed. At high tide keep to the path along the dunes.

Near the far end there is a sunken track (Sea Tangle Road) coming down to the sands; turn up this (with care!), then, after 130 yards, turn right along a fence to go round Chapel Ness. Note how the trees have been planed by the wind. A grassy track (where cowslips grow) leads along outside a tall wall to open up a view over the reef of East Vows and out to the

Bass Rock. The beacon didn't prevent a ship, *Vulcan*, running onto the rocks in 1882 with its load of pig iron. But what was a boat from Middlesbrough to Grangemouth doing there at all? The gable is all that remains of an eleventh-century pilgrim chapel, where pilgrims rested after their ferry crossing from Dunbar en route to St Andrews. As many as 10,000 a year made the hazardous crossing. Macduff, thane of Fife, is thought to have built a chapel in 1093 as an offering to the ferrymen who rowed him over to safety after Macbeth had slaughtered his family at his East Wemyss castle in 1054. The Reformation rather killed off pilgrimages, and the easier, safer ferries at Pettycur, Burntisland or Queensferry grew in importance. Steamers once operated Leith-Elie-North Berwick, till World War I brought their end.

An open grassy area gives a view along the Elie seafront with its colourful sands. We head in to walk along Earlsferry High Street. Note the fancy iron brackets holding some gutters. The town hall (1872) has the clock tower with a sailing ship weather vane. The house opposite has a sundial with several faces on its west skew putt. A plaque by the town hall door commemorates James Braid, a local golfer, who won the Open *five times* in the years 1901-10. Polish forces are commemorated on a wall plaque. All along the coast broad Fife accents can belong to surnames like Matyssek or Peplinska, for many stayed on and married local lassies. 'Wynd' is a euphoric word for lane: Glovers Wynd, Castwell Wynd, Cadger's (Carrier's) Wynd and Cross Wynd are on our route, the last presumably once the mercat cross site. Two-way traffic resumes after Ferry Road.

The High Street goes on with no break past Williamsburgh and Liberty to **Elie** (they were separate burghs till 1929). After Liberty turn up Golf Club Lane, which leads to the Elie Sports Club complex. The Pavilion Café by the tennis courts may be welcome. But the main interest is over to the left beyond the golf club house: a hut with a long tube rising from it. This is the starters' hut for Elie Golf Course, and because the first drive is blind, in 1966 they installed the periscope from a 1954 submarine *Excalibur* to see if the fairway ahead was free. *Excalibur* was an experimental submarine powered by hydrogen peroxide, an idea superseded by nuclear power.

Return to the linear route which now becomes Links Place. An attractive modern development has a mural carving of a boat. In the past (and the nickname has been retained) this was jokingly called 'the Sahara Park', no doubt from sand perpetually blowing off the beach. Turn down right into Fountain Road, which leads to South Street, and a view of the popular holiday beach. This was the original High Street of the royal burgh where several ancient buildings survive. Gillespie House (left) has a faint 1682 lintel for Alex Gillespie and Christina Small. The doorway (the 'muckle yett') with a ruined sundial over it is the remains of a sawpit for timber imported from the Baltic. On the seaward side the Castle is fifteenth-century, the town house of the Gourlays, related to the Sharps, one of whom, the hated Archbishop, was murdered as he rode in his carriage to St Andrews.

Turn left up School Wynd to reach the main crossroads of Elie, as one could gather from the meeting of School Wynd, High Street, Bank Street and Park Place. Opposite is the war memorial (looking like a gateway) while the churchyard entrance is along a bit, the old session house with odd finials. The baker on the corner sells *sair heids* (sore heads).

The church is quite dominant, built in the early seventeenth century, but the tower added in 1726. There are only three faces to the clock as, when installed in 1900, there was no town on the fourth side. When the clock was renewed the workings went to Edinburgh, where they still drive the works of Princes Street's famous floral clock. The church is a typical T-shape, with the pulpit central and facing the laird's loft. A major

Elie Church.

The Granary and Elie Harbour.

addition, when the church united with the Wood Memorial Church, was the addition of their Burne-Jones windows.

The graveyard is mostly Victorian, but some earlier stones have been placed at the east end of the church (outside). One seems to be a skeleton, 'rolled up in a carpet', so all that shows are skull, stark ribs and feet. This commemorates a daughter of Turnbull of Bogmill (d.1650) whose large decorative slab also stands against the wall. The bull's head, turned aside, is a pun on the family name.

At a meeting of paths by the east porch is a stone inscribed to Charles Fox Cattanach, wife (*sic*) of James Smith, Ship Master… and James Smith her (*sic*) husband'. Apparently the minister mixed up names at the christening and the superstitious family insisted the girl went through life with her male Christian name. There used to be a 'lang grave' for a drowned sailor found on the shore with arms outstretched, and superstition forbade the breaking of the arms to fit a conventional grave. A sorry number of stones testify to the dangers of the sea. One accident happened in full view of family and friends when a boat was fishing between the harbour and the ferry chapel on an apparently calm day, only to be overturned by a squall. One widow gave birth to a girl a few days later and she was given her father's name, Andrew. One woman lost husband, brother and brother-in-law.

The masons building the church inserted a black stone as a safeguard against witches, a real horror, in Fife and the Lothians mainly, with an estimated 4,400 women burnt as witches between 1590 and 1680. It was hardly a peaceful century, nor the time perhaps to be erecting a church. When the English Civil War broke out in England, Scott of Ardross, the laird, went off to support King Charles while the Scots parliament and church opposed him. The Elie minister went south too, so was opposing his own patron. Scott was captured at the Battle of Worcester and lost his estates. The Anstruthers became the new owners, having played their war games a bit more successfully. Balcaskie House, inland, is still in the Anstruther family.

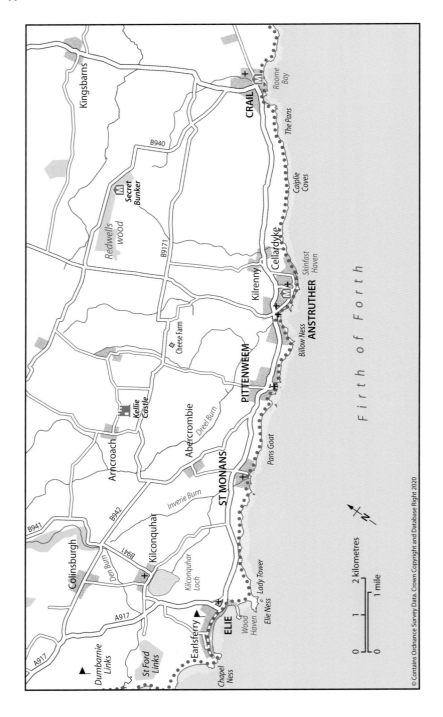

Kingsbarns

CRAIL

Roome
Bay

B940

The Pans

Secret
Bunker

Caplie
Coves

Redwells
wood

B9171

Cellardyke

Skinfast
Haven

Kilrenny

ANSTRUTHER

Cheese Farm

Billow Ness

Kellie
Castle

PITTENWEEM

Abercrombie

Dreel Burn

Arncroach

Pans Goat

ST MONANS

B942

Inverie Burn

B941

Kilconquhar

Colinsburgh

Den Burn

B941

Kilconquhar
Loch

Lady Tower

A917

ELIE

Elie Ness

Wood
Haven

Earlsferry

Dumbarnie
Links

St Ford
Links

Chapel
Ness

A917

Firth of Forth

N

2 kilometres

1

1 mile

0

0

© Contains Ordnance Survey Data. Crown Copyright and Database Right 2020

VI
The East Neuk
O.S. 59 / 371

From Elie Ness (Point) back to Pettycur (Kinghorn) we have really been coasting round a huge bay made up of smaller bays. The East Neuk has a much more open aspect, with the feeling of sea rather than estuary. Out in the sea the Isle of May (see Appendix 4) catches the eye with the 'lump and cone' of Bass Rock and North Berwick Law on the far shore. As much time can vanish exploring the towns, 'strung like pearls', as can walking the thread of paths linking them; you can stop, start and use transport at will rather than being strictly programmed. The towns are only one to three miles apart and all are well-geared for tourist needs. Crail is between 10 and 11 miles ahead.

We still have some of **Elie** to view as we set off. Continue along the High Street past the garden (Toll Green), then turn right down to the sea. The curving road is known as the Toft. Admiralty Lane, left, is our continuation, but a walk out along the 1586 harbour arm may appeal first. The big building is the Granary, now turned into flats, beyond the clutter of watersports centre and sailing club. There a viewpoint indicator on a knoll. The local sailing club's first Hon. Commodore was Admiral Sir William James, who is known much better as the boy in the painting, 'Bubbles', used in Pears Soap advertising. Their first boat was called *Bubbles*. The ill-fated Earl of Mar landed at Elie before going on to raise the standard at Braemar to start the 1715 Jacobite rebellion.

Head up Admiralty Lane and on to the start of Wadeslea, from where a field edge path leads to the parking/picnic/toilet area on the bay of Wood Haven. Wood Haven is more often called Ruby Bay (the rubies were garnets) and ends at a prow overlooking the 1908 lighthouse: a pair of battlemented towers, one square, one round, which are actually on a small island. David Stevenson supervised this light's erection in 1908. Carbide gas lighting has long gone and the light is now automatic. A Russian schooner *Jupiter*, sailing from Alloa to Riga with coal, 'took the ground' off Elie Ness in 1897. Five crew were saved by breeches buoy, but the mate and captain refused to leave their doomed ship. A month later a salvage

The coast at Ardross.

lighter, *Grangemouth*, was anchored over the sunken schooner and, in only a force 7, went ashore too and now lies alongside *Jupiter*.

The grassy path swings towards an obvious tower, the Lady Tower, built c.1760 and named after Lady Janet Anstruther, 'a coquette and a beauty' according to Carlyle, who liked to swim in the sea and had a tower and grotto changing room below built to satisfy her whim. A bellman was sent through the town to warn plebs to keep away. The tower is still a good viewpoint.

Our path heads along marram-held dunes above the typical warm-coloured sands. Elie House lies inland and the trees there are beginning to take on that wind-planed appearance that becomes more and more obvious as we head east till trees themselves almost disappear. Nearing Ardross note the basalt dyke that runs down the shore like a man-made wall. The path wiggles on and the rock is suddenly tawny sandstone, so the next stretch of bay has 'silver sands' as against the 'golden sands' of the East Links back the way. At low tide the ragged reefs reach out to sea one after the other (volcanic rock, more resistant than the sedimentary between).

The path wends through ruinous Ardross Castle, erected in 1370 by Sir William Dishington, sheriff of Fife. His father, also Sir William, had married Robert the Bruce's sister Elizabeth. On reaching the castle an eighteenth-century rectangular lectern-style doocot can be seen near the main road. Our path leads down, passing a filled-in railway bridge, to a bay where proper embanking had been made to protect the line. The views expand, both ahead to the Isle of May and back to the Lady Tower.

Newark Castle is approached by a steep path up left. There's a post on the shore and a notice warns that if the sea reaches it an alternative route on from the castle may be advisable. This heads directly inland to a track, then, before a house, turns right to follow a long field edge to an isolated one-time railway bridge with a small span over the Inweary (St Monans) Burn and a larger arch for a path to the A917. Follow the burn down to the sea at St Monans Church to join the *voie normale*.

Newark Castle is a gaunt spectacle, its local sandstone badly weathered, more impressive for its setting than its architectural interest. Little remains apart from the four walls and a row of vaulted cells. Last century Sir Robert Lorimer produced a grand plan for restoring the castle for Sir William Burrell, the shipping magnate. Had this gone ahead the Burrell Collection could well have been here! The castle was bought by Fifer David Leslie in 1649, and it was from this building he took his title, Earl of Newark, the reward for finally defeating 'the great Montrose' at the Battle of Philiphaugh (where prisoners were massacred afterwards in the other Newark Castle). Just beyond the castle is its sixteenth-century beehive doocot, weathered, but complete, perched on a prow above the sea. A gate by the doocot leads us on, swooping downwards, then along towards the church. Just short of it we are diverted down some steps to walk along the foot of a high wall to reach the inlet with a slip and the Inweary Burn. This rather minor challenge is the cause of the long inland high tide option, whereas in the past one just stepped over the kirkyard wall to reach the church, which should be visited if open.

St Monans has seen something of a rejuvenation since the shipyard works closed in 1993 and is now the smallest and most colourful of the the East Neuk towns. It often appears, less accurately, as St Monance. Before the cult of the saint it was Inverie or Inweary. The church dates back to *c*.1265 and stands by the Inweary (St Monans) Burn. We enter by a door (with a posthole) into what is the original south transept, and the pulpit and communion table are at the crossing, facing the chancel—so in pre-Reformation days the altar would be at the far end. Surprisingly, sacramental niches, piscina and sedila have survived. An older model ship (eighteenth-century) and one of a fishing boat hang in the church, whitewashed and plain as the interior is. Display boards give plenty of information.

David II was largely responsible for rebuilding the church in 1346, Dishington, the laird, picking up the bill. Legends conflict as to why the king undertook this work: one says he was hit by two arrows at the Battle of Neville's Cross and at St Monan's shrine one of the shafts 'leapt out of the wound', the other says he was crossing the Forth to Ardross Castle, was caught in a storm, and made the vow to build a church if saved. The English burnt the church in 1544, but in 1646 it was made the local parish church. In the 1950s it had to be rescued from decay and heavy-handed Victorian alterations. It has always been a sea-mark but, oddly, there is no weathercock.

The ragged formation offshore is named the Boiling Cauldron, and can echo and boom dramatically in the surf. Legend says witches were thrown into the sea to gain a good catch. Fishermen have always been both godly and superstitious.

St Monans' Kirk.

St Monans.

No boat would leave a Fife port if a pig, a cat, a minister or
a female was encountered when preparing for sea. Certain
words also were never to be uttered, including names with
double consonants, such as Watt, Ross, Marr. Any potential
fear was allayed by touching iron (not wood). An extreme
case was noted at Charlestown. A sloop, laden with lime,
was ready to sail but stayed weatherbound for two weeks.
(You can see why rail superseded sail.) When the wind at last
changed the crew made all ready to sail as soon as the skipper
arrived. He, however, shook his head. No. He had run into a
woman on the way down.

John Paul Jones keeps appearing. He was a Kirkcudbright
youth who proved a brilliant seaman and became one of new
America's first heroes. In British history books of course he is
a villain. When he made his raid on the Forth he kidnapped a
St Monans man as pilot, but he proved so ineffective he had
to be replaced. Jones' most famous quote was in a 1799 battle when his ship was sinking under him and he was hailed
about surrendering. He shouted back, 'I have not yet begun

to fight'. His remit, as an American captain, was to 'distress' the enemy, which he did with élan.

Leaving St Monan's church, cross the burn and go up between houses opposite. A narrow footpath/steps climbs up to come out on a road (Braehead) from which take the right fork to drop down again. Continue along attractive West Shore and walk through the West End, coming out to the harbour at a big slip, a reminder of a shipbuilding past. (Note the Welly Boot Garden.) The Miller family began boat building here in 1747, a business which lasted over 200 years and a big economic blow when it closed. The two outer harbour arms were built by the Stevenson family, the central pier was assisted by nationwide donations to help local poverty. Mid Shore leads to the eastern side of the harbour, with several wynds leading off into quite a maze of period houses, with fore-stairs, crowstep gables, pantiles, harled walls and so on, which would repay a wander. St Monans Heritage Collection is housed beside a pillared fore-stair. Several buildings are NTS restorations. Opposite the mine (where there's a collecting box) Station Road has the welcoming Diving Gannet café. Continue by Mid Shore to reach the Eastern Harbour with its slip and smokery. Landward is the attractive Virgin Square. I had to ask in the end as to where I could see the zigzag breakwater in

The zigzag breakwater, St Monans. See if you can find it.
(J. K. Querido.)

the picture. Can you find it? St Monans was home in the film *The Railway Man* and used for the remake of *Whisky Galore.*

Don't head off along East Shore, which would seem the obvious way on, but head up (along Forth Street) then first right, to Rose Street, from which a clear path will take us on to Pittenweem. The **windmill** ahead is the main attraction *en route*. A path leads up to it from a grassy recreational area and outdoor pool (opened in 1937 but no longer maintained). There are excellent description boards about the salt industry. There's a garden picnic area below the windmill. The windmill pumped sea water up to the salt pans. In the eighteenth century Sir John Anstruther opened new coal pits for the salt pans, which were connected to Pittenweem by a wagonway. A major underground fire in 1794 caused a slump, and the salt pans were abandoned by 1823. You can still see the holding tank between tidelines and the cut where the water was piped up. Inland, the farm is called Coal Farm. We now look *across* to the Bass Rock and the Law, while, back the way, we can still see the Lady Tower. As we continue, a stream rushing down is the chalybeate well of St Monans, so iron-impregnated that the fishermen washed their nets in its staining water to make them more durable.

Easy walking leads us on and, when the path forks, take the left branch, to gain the prow above, where there's a shelter, benches, crazy golf and car park. Down at sea level concrete arms indicate a bathing area dating back to before World War I. Start down from the shelter—and suddenly **Pittenweem** is in view. A row of houses (West Shore) rims a quiet bay, a corner few visitors see. There was once a gas works bang in the middle and the slip was probably to supply the works with coal. Houses must have found the sea wall little defence in big storms. The wall was tarred as a protection. Spur stones mark the opening past the last house—and we come to the wider Mid Shore.

A reef on the right makes an almost natural slip and is a good viewpoint. On the left the house with a pend (passage) is the Cooperage, an indication of its past use. Pittenweem's main use today is as the coast's home fishing port (a port was first mentioned in 1228), and the frequent KY registration stands for Kirkcaldy. Boat names are as varied and interesting as house names. The fish market stands over to the right at the harbour, protected by a long arm, the end of which (with a harbour light) is an unusual viewpoint for Pittenweem. Fife has fascinating place names and an anonymous rhyme suggests, 'Largo, Blebo, Dunino/ Into Europe seem to go,/ But plainly Scottish we may deem/ Auchtermuchty, Pittenweem.'

An ice cream parlour (Janetta's; famous St Andrews product) may be welcome. There is a range of eateries here, and up in the town.

All the wynds deserve exploration but we will have to be selective. Cove Wynd (it should be Cave Wynd) lies up from the mine collection box and has the historical feature of St Fillan's Cave. Pittenweem appears on a charter of David I as Pit-ne-weme: *the place of the cave*. The cave is locked, but a key can be obtained, as noted, at places on the High Street. The church is at the top of Cove Wynd and its key can be found at the chemists in Market Street, a bit further along the High Street.

While fetching keys note the Kelly Lodging halfway along the High Street (landward side), once the town house of the Earls of Kellie, with corbelled turret and other sixteenth-century features. Walking back the church dominates the view, the tower looking very like the tolbooth it once was. Against the wall is the shaft of the mercat cross. The bell was cast in 1663 for 'Joran Puttensen's widow' and is Swedish. Just left of the gate into the churchyard, among the good selection

West Shore, Pittenweem ('tideline houses').

Pittenweem.

of seventeenth-century table stones, is one with an anything but modest inscription (to David Binning *d*.1675).

Seaward of the church are the scant ruins of an Augustinian Priory where the monks based on the rather threatened Isle of May were granted a site near the already famous cave. St Fillan was a seventh-century missionary, so the cave, still laid out as a chapel, is one of Scotland's oldest religious sites. There's a well in the left inner chamber and a stair leads up to a chamber 10m. overhead in the Priory garden.

Having returned the keys, descend School Wynd (first wynd westwards) back to the harbour and walk towards the east end, where the much-photographed houses of the Gyles (restored by NTS) look on the outer harbour. *The Winter Guest* film (starring Emma Thompson) made use of the Gyles and the Pittenweem scenery generally. The three-storey house is a sea captain's home of 1626. One Pittenweem captain took Charles II to France after the Battle of Worcester in 1651.

In 1705 three women died and many others were tortured on a witchcraft charge based on the accusations of a teenager. One of the three died after five months of torture and incarceration, another starved to death in her cell, the third escaped only to be caught and lynched by a mob who dragged her to the harbour and swung her over the water to be stoned, then crushed her under a door over which a horse and cart were driven back and forth.

The Gyles, Pittenweem.

Pittenweem has an annual Arts Festival each August, when over 40 sites (from Kelly Lodging to rooms in houses) have exhibitions. Gardens are also open and cafés appear in back gardens and terraces over the sea. Of its kind it is one of the happiest festivals. Too far inland if afoot, but worth visiting, is the NTS Kellie Castle and Garden, restored by Sir Robert Lorimer last century. The garden is a noted organic showpiece.

But to push on eastwards; from the Gyles head well up Abbey Wall Road and when the brae swings left, take a wall opening, right, to go through a play area and off along the cliff top behind a housing scheme. The strong diagonal strata out to sea is, ominously, the Break Boats. The cliff is badly eroded. Down to the shore again, follow the edge of Anstruther golf course, the only real gap between the towns. (One small bay is heaped with cockle shells.) Anstruther ('Ainster' locally) is an incorporation of four old royal burghs: Anstruther Wester and Easter, Cellardyke and Kilrenny—a link-up rather contrasting with Buckhaven, Denbeath, Methil and Leven. There is not much to see along the way: the concrete box is an old anti-aircraft gun site, there's a lookout post (closed) and another forgotten rock bathing pool at Billow Ness. In 1935 a coal boat went aground offshore and swimmers found amusement in swimming out to the stranded boat.

At the grassy point of Billow Ness we gain a good view to **Anstruther**. The offshore jut of rock (with a marker post) is Johnny Doo's Pulpit, but it has an entirely historical ecclesiastical connection, for the young local lad, Thomas Chalmers, came here to practice his sermons. He was licensed to preach by St Andrews Presbytery at the age of 19, but then studied mathematics at Edinburgh before an appointment at St Andrews. He later became minister at Kilmany (Fife's), and Glasgow (first the Tron, then St John's) where his preaching drew large crowds and his work for the poor was outstanding. The century-old fight against patronage was coming to a head, and in 1843 Chalmers was a leader in the Disruption, when nearly half the Church of Scotland ministers walked out rather than tolerate the undemocratic and often misused system— an incredible act of faith and defiance, for the ministers lost church, manse and salary at a stroke, and often had difficulty in establishing new churches, the landowners being anything but helpful. Congregations sometimes had to meet between the tidelines, and there was a floating church in the west.

The battlemented tower up on the golf course is the local war memorial. Nets protect walkers from golf balls, though, I suspect, these were erected to stop sliced drives ending in the sea. The course is 9 holes, in an attractive setting. The clubhouse was given by an officer who fought at Trafalgar. Pass it, along Shore Road, turning left into Crichton Street, to reach the A917. (Several B & Bs lie left, on the Pittenweem road.) We turn right to follow the High Street (of **Anstruther Wester**), passing the Dreel Tavern, where a plaque mentions one of the stories of the Guid Man o' Ballengeich, as James V was called on his anonymous wanderings. There was no bridge over the Dreel Burn then and he was naturally carried over by a gaberlunzie (beggar) woman who, instead of the expected pittance, was paid in gold.

As the main road turns sharply to cross the Dreel Burn, note the seventeenth-century house on the corner, covered in seashells, the work of one Alex Batchelor, an eccentric slater. Buckie House (buckie in the loose sense of shell, not one species) has parts harled with shells, and the main front is highly decorative with a triple frieze of scallop shells at

Crossing the Dreel Burn, Anstruther.

the top. Batchelor used to charge a penny to let people see his coffin, which was also decorated with shells. For a half penny he would lie in it (in 1863 he was buried in it).

Across the road is an obviously old church (with the traditional creamy wash), now the parish church hall, while, beside it, on the Esplanade (the lane leading off seawards at the bad bend) is the eighteenth-century town hall. In the thirteenth century it is said an iron basket on top of the tower was lit as a beacon to guide shipping in to harbour. The weathervane is a salmon, and the church was dedicated in 1243 to St Nicholas, patron saint of the sea. The graveyard has superb sea views—and some interesting stones, including a very early one dated 1598 now set in the wall. The tablet next to it has good Biblical Scots on it (Yat is *yett*, a gate).

In behind the building, beside the road, is a stone coffin (empty!) with a clear covering, for a Rev. James Forester, 1791. On the wall behind is a slab with a poem by Andrew Greig (2003). The hall is named after the church's second minister, Hew Scott, who spent his summers visiting 900 churches to write up details of all the incumbents back to the Reformation, gathered in the volumes of the *Fasti Ecclesiae Scoticanae*.

East, over the burn, is the one-time historic Smugglers Inn. If the tide is well out, go down the Esplanade. If the tide is full, still go down the Esplanade but then come back and on to Anster East. At low tide ancient stepping stones allow you to cross the mouth of the burn—hence the options.

The Esplanade (odd name, for it isn't) has several good buildings. A plaque at the start commemorates John Keay, a local lad who became captain of the *Ariel* and other clipper ships. The *Ariel* and *Taeping* (built for Captain Rodger of Cellardyke) took part in the most famous tea clipper race of all time in 1866. After 99 days at sea, both came in to the Thames (from Foochow in China) on the same tide! (*Ariel* had Anster crew, *Taeping* lads from Cellardyke.) Several houses are visibly dated, and the wheatsheaf on an old cottage may point to its having been an inn. Steps lead down to the big stepping stones across the Dreel Burn to **Anstruther** itself.

Across the river once stood Dreel Castle, where Mary Queen of Scots slept and Charles II gave his hosts the back-handed compliment for his supper: 'Aye, no a bad bite for a craw's nest'. The row of houses (Castle Street) leads us to Shore Street, the heart of the Anstruthers.

If having to avoid the Dreel Burn and crossing by the A917, note the plaque on the bridge marking a 1795 rebuilding of the 1630 bridge. (There's also been an 1831 remodelling.) The Smugglers Inn (now housing) was an old coaching inn, but the name no doubt was justified, and would be anywhere on this coast. Keep on, right, a narrowing of the High Street. An FCP sign takes us down Wightman's Wynd to the seafront. Down the next wynd, Old Post Office Close, is the house where Chalmers was born, old long before then, with ships' masts and timbers used as roof beams. The big red sandstone building on the front was the 1908 Murray Library (style: 'fussy Renaissance'); Murray was a local lad who made good trading with Australia. It is now a hostel (tel: 01333 311123). Across from here, sited by the bus stop, is the 1677 mercat cross. As at Pittenweem a walk out on the harbour arm gives a good view of the handsome town frontage. The light is the Chalmers Memorial Lighthouse, an 1880 gift, as was the first lifeboat in 1865, from a Cheltenham lady who never visited Anstruther. The Chalmers Memorial Church steeple for long dominated the view to the town, and was a useful sea mark on this low, featureless coast, but vandals in 1991 set fire to the unused church which had to be demolished.

Though bigger than Pittenweem, Anstruther's eight-eenth-century harbour lost its fishing eminence and is now a super-marina. Robert Louis Stevenson lived here while his father was enlarging the harbour in 1860. At that time he was expected to follow the family business of lighthouse and har-bour building, and had not yet made his break for literature. He was to apologise: 'Though I haunted the breakwater by day and even loved the place for the sake of the sunshine, the thrilling seaside air, the wash of the waves on the sea-face, the green glimmer of the divers' helmets far below, and the musical clinking of the masons, my one genuine preoccupation lay elsewhere, and my only industry was in the hours when I was not on duty'.

Sailings to the Isle of May (3 hours ashore) leave from here during the summer, either on the characterful *May Princess* or by one of the RIBs, *Osprey* or *Osprey II*. These are exciting but noisy and brash and the *May Princess* is more suitable for experiencing the natural world. A place might be booked at the office hut near sailing time but departures are often full. Book ahead (07957 585200 or *www.isleofmayferry.com*).

At the east end of Shore Street is the Scottish Fisheries Museum, a major attraction and one of the best. (The café may be welcome too.) The building is on St Ayles land which has recorded connections with the fishing industry in 1318. The laird of 'Anstroyir' then made over rights to Balmerino Abbey, including the erection of fishing booths and drying nets. A chapel was built in the fifteenth century, but the site has been 'recycled' several times over, including for its apt present use, opening in 1969. There is a wide range of exhibits and re-creations, a working wheelhouse, a collection of boats and much else. Allow plenty of time for a visit.

The Battle of Kilsyth in 1645 saw so many local men slain

that it is blamed for a decline in East Neuk fortunes. In 1670 a storm devastated harbours and houses too, and the 1707 Union brought no benefit: in that year the Ainsters had 30 boats, in 1764 there were 5. Over-fishing (by both home and foreign boats) saw the herring industry die.

At the end of the museum buildings go through a narrow wynd (Whale Close) to East Green, where there's a plaque to Captain John Smith, skipper of *Min* and *Lahloo* in the tea clipper days. He was drowned when his ship was lost with all hands off the Hebrides

In the Scottish Fisheries Museum, Anstruther.

in 1874. The town's famous school, Waid Academy, was endowed by a Royal Navy officer, Andrew Waid (1736–1803). You can't escape sea connections in Anstruther. A William Smith was one notable whaler for whom Smith Sound in the Arctic is named. He brought back the biggest jawbones of a whale ever caught—and which stood on East Forth Street for many years. Head back westwards to where East Green meets Haddfoot, a stey brae which justifies 'Hadd-the-feet!' (Watch your feet!) On it, left, there is some decoration owing its moulding to egg boxes. Behind gates lies a big house (Johnstone House) which was once the home of a Tahitian princess. She had married a Scots merchant, and when he died she married an employee, George Darsie, who brought her 'home'. The house was bought by a son-in-law solicitor, and he added a ballroom for his fun-loving wife who, widowed, had to sell out to a half-sister. She'd cannily married a minister whose main reading was the *Financial Times,* and who made a fortune.

Scottish merchants often fell foul of the Inquisition in Spain and were imprisoned or burnt as heretics, so there was something of an about turn when the ships of the Spanish Armada came to grief. A party of 260 Spaniards from Medina's *El Gran Grifon* somehow made their way from the Northern Isles to Anstruther, much to the consternation of the people. (A local recalled their poor shape: 'many berdless, sillie, trauchled and houngred'.) James Melville, the redoubtable local minister, could speak Spanish and made his opinions plain but, nevertheless, Scottish folk succoured *any* in distress. The Spaniards were given hospitality until repatriated. This paid off, for later, when an Anstruther ship was seized in Spain and it came to the notice of Medina who rescued men and ship from the Inquisition, and entertained the men, in return for their good turn at Anstruther. Melville's Manse still exists.

Heading on we enter the lang toon of **Cellardyke,** which is so overshadowed by Anstruther to which it was attached in 1929. Keep along the shore road by the Sun Tavern, passing the two green leading lights and then swinging right. New houses, Harbour Lea, left, have been highly praised. The main road swings inland, but we keep on along the road parallel to the sea all the way through Cellardyke. This is James Street (not mentioned initially) which runs along to Tolbooth Wynd, the original tolbooth replaced by the 1883 municipal building, against which is the surviving shaft of the 1642 mercat cross.

The QE2 off Cellardyke Harbour.

Our shore road now becomes John Street, then George Street, where a plaque recalls an otherwise forgotten rhymester, 'Poetry Peter' (Smith). The open space of the harbour area comes as a contrast, but the harbour is barely used now. The older name was Skinfast Haven. An offshore reef is Cuttyskelly. Telford's fellow engineer, Joseph Mitchell, rebuilt an earlier harbour dating away back. In the mid-nineteenth century a small Greenland whaling company operated from here but lost out to bigger Dundee boats. A cod-liver-oil factory has also gone. Just past the end of the harbour a house called Taeping commemorates Captain Alexander Rodger, a local fisherman who became captain and then owner of several clippers, *Min*, *Lahloo* and *Taeping* among the more famous. (His fisherman father had died at the Burntisland drave—the annual herring fishing—in 1814.) One of his contemporaries was Walter Hughes who roamed many seas, ran opium from China to Siam till too risky, started a sheep-run the size of Fife in Australia, found copper, and became the richest man in Australia, which bought respectability, so he retired with a knighthood.

I once used Cellardyke harbour to launch my canoe and paddle out to circumnavigate the QE2. She was anchored there so passengers could be taken by ferry and bus to see the Millennium Open at St Andrews (Tiger Woods won by 8 strokes). This last great Scottish-built liner would travel 6 million miles and go round the world 25 times. She is now berthed in Dubai as a hotel.

The Braes and Town Green now flank to the inland side of us, on the right a row of tidily-restored houses; one, the Cooperage, has craft symbols carved on the corner. Barrel-making in 1833 employed 70 coopers, as an example of how big this trade once was. Cellardyke alone had 24 breweries. Cellardyke folk were no more thirsty than anywhere else; beer was simply the everyday drink in those days. Tea was the luxury (strange role-reversal). The stone on the corner shows the tools of this trade, which the tea clippers presumably helped to kill off. The Town Green was a gift from Captain Rodger.

Cellardyke rather peters out: there's a children's play area, the war memorial up on the Braes and another forgotten tidal pool before the final car park. (The rocks beyond the pool are the Cardinal's Steps, where the newly created prelate, Cardinal Beaton, went aboard his barge to travel to St Andrews in style.) The caravan park surrounds what was Kilrenny Mill. Kilrenny itself, only a hamlet, lies up on the A917 and we only glimpse a St Monan's-like spire as we walk on. The spire too was a good sea mark and, oddly, many fishermen lived up in Kilrenny. Cellardyke was often called Nether Kilrenny. We follow a track right by the shore. **Caiplie** Farm (converted to flats) is unusual, being at shore level rather than up on a raised-beach level. There's an octagonal (pantiled) wheelhouse, another east coast feature. Fossil tree stumps can be found on the shore. The Isle of May shows its steepest profile and is at its nearest to shore. The twins of Bass and Law lie beyond.

On we come to the stark feature known as the Caiplie Coves, a sea-carving of caves on the 8m. raised beach, multi-hued and weathered into fantastic shapes. The main cave (Chapel Cave) has several incised crosses dating back to early Christian days, when missionaries such as Adrian may have lived here. The Covenanter Alexander Peden once used its shelter, and early last century the cave was taken over by 'Covey Jimmy', Jimmy Gilligan from Aberdeen who served in the Boer War, Afghanistan and elsewhere, spoke French

Caiplie Coves.

and Latin but, hating city life, set up home here in 1910. The coast becomes rougher. At the Millport Burn there are yellow flags and the celery-like dropwort which is best avoided—it was a popular medieval poison! A ruined cottage, tucked in a bay, was a salmon bothy. Saltworks, dating back to c.1700, explain the name, the Pans. Later there were brickworks, some ruins of which remain. The walking is probably the loneliest on the coast till now, and quite atmospheric some find with the sweeping sea views. The Isle of May is now astern of us! A pull up a prow brings Crail into near view, and we dip down and then up again to reach the historic town.

The shoreline is impractical, so the path rises up to go round the cliffs into **Crail**—and, doing so, gives classic views down to the tiny, tidy harbour. Turn right at the tarmac, but when the road swings left, continue on a footpath which will lead out to the main coast road. Turn right, passing the leading lights for the harbour (one above, one below the A917). Opposite Lomond Terrace (church on the corner) turn right for a path that leads steeply down to the harbour, 'the Hens Ladder'.

Crail is the most photographed or painted harbour along the East Neuk coast and the quiet state now with just a few boats going after lobsters or partans hardly makes it seem to have been the most important at one time. (Robert the Bruce granted its charter as a Royal Burgh in 1310.) Most of the buildings round the harbour are seventeenth-century. The west arm of the harbour was built by Robert Stevenson in 1826. The painted town arms on a plaque on the largest building points to the old customs house. Read any notices and wander out on the far, encircling harbour arm for the view. The gasworks on the bay beside the harbour was removed in 1960. Coal was once dug out of open workings at Crail, and a Queen Mary coin was once found by the miners in old workings. Crail never industrialised, as it lacked burns for giving water power. Grain and farm produce increased its exports when the Forth & Clyde Canal was opened. While ships took heavy cargoes like coal and salt to the Low Countries they needed ballast for the return voyage and filled with red roof tiles—hence the pantiles of the East Neuk. (They also brought back Delft pottery, silks and spices.)

The sandy bay beyond the harbour ends at a long sea-ward-running reef, then there's a short reach of sand and

Crail Harbour, from the Braes.

Crail Harbour.

boulders, another reef, and beyond this is an obvious angled slab at the foot of the shaly cliff. A fossil tree will be found at that spot, the stump as if sawn off above the spreading roots, while various pieces of trunk lie around.

From the harbour, head up Shoregate with its attractive old houses. St Adrian's, named after the early missionary, has blue shutters and a half-figure over the door. Go up the steps (as the road bends) to follow airy Castle Walk. One looks down on St Adrian's garden and Maggie Inglis' Hole as this bit of coast is called. There's an old sundial and view indicator on the corner. The castle has long gone. The building at the end of Castle Walk was a watch house, dated 1782.

Once there turn left up a short road with garages on the left, but, first, briefly, turn down right to read the display telling about the King's Mills which once stood here. Turn into Rumford which leads on to the wide Nethergate, which with Market Street, were the well-planned extensions when the town spread out from the harbour area. (Hotels and B & Bs are to be found on the Nethergate.) Cross over to pass the row of cottages, restored by the NTS under its Little Houses scheme. The last has the lower floor corner cut in to allow traffic to pass; go through this gap and turn sharp left to walk towards the Crail Pottery (worth a visit) then turn right up Rose Wynd which leads to the High Street.

Turn right to come on the old tolbooth which shows a strong Dutch influence (and a Dutch bell, dated 1520, which,

Crail Tolbooth.

till recently, rang a curfew at 22.00). The weather vane is a
Crail capon. The building now holds the library and local
council offices. Beside it is the Crail Museum and Heritage
Centre. At the tolbooth corner with the flagpole is a *loupin
on stane* (a mounting block to assist riders onto horseback).

Along wide Marketgate from the tolbooth is a granite fountain commemorating Queen Victoria's Diamond Jubilee (1897)
and the reconstructed mercat cross of which only the shaft
is old. The markets, dating back to Robert the Bruce's time,
were held on Sundays until the Reformation. There are many
fine seventeenth and eighteenth-century town houses as we
walk along eastwards. One marriage lintel is dated 1619, the
earliest we've met. At the corner for the church gates at the
far end of Marketgate is an erratic boulder, the Blue Stone,
which tradition has it, came from the Isle of May. The devil
had taken a scunner to Crail kirk folk and threw a big stone
at the place; splitting in the air, one piece went flying on to
Balcomie, while this piece came very near hitting the church.

That would have been a pity, for Crail Kirk is hoary with
history. Dedicated to St Maelrubha of Applecross in 1243, it
later became St Mary's and also a collegiate church. Knox
preached here and James Sharp (later archbishop) was one
of its ministers. Proximity to St Andrews meant frequent
involvement in church and state affairs. Major alterations
were made in 1796, 1815 and 1963, the tower is thirteenth-century, and inside there are quite a few features of note: early
carved oak panels, a painted panel from the sailors' loft and
a restored thirteenth-century lancet window with beautiful
modern glass, more recent glass in the tower and a rather
worn Pictish stone moved from near Fife Ness. The tower has
grooves where mediaeval archers sharpened their arrow tips.

The kirkyard has a unique number of early mural monuments, some sixteenth-century. Behind the church there is a
mort-house where bodies were kept locked up till decayed
beyond use to body snatchers. A tablet informs, 'Erected for
securing the dead'. On a cheerier note the east side of the
graveyard and Denburn Wood beyond become massed with
snowdrops in the spring. From the rear of the churchyard
walk down Denburn Wood (Rude Well) and return to the
Marketgate.

Crail's name is given variously on old maps. One I've
seen had Carell and, on the same map, backtracking, would
you recognise Sandness (Pittenweem), Leauins Mouth, Kirk

Caldey, Pretticur, Kinghorne and Brunt Iland? The town had, and has, a feeling of being somewhat apart. In the eighteenth century a Glaswegian asked a friend if he had been to America, and had the reply,'No, but I've a brother who has been to Crail'. It is a good place to pause before the inescapable longest and hardest length of walking the Fife Coast.

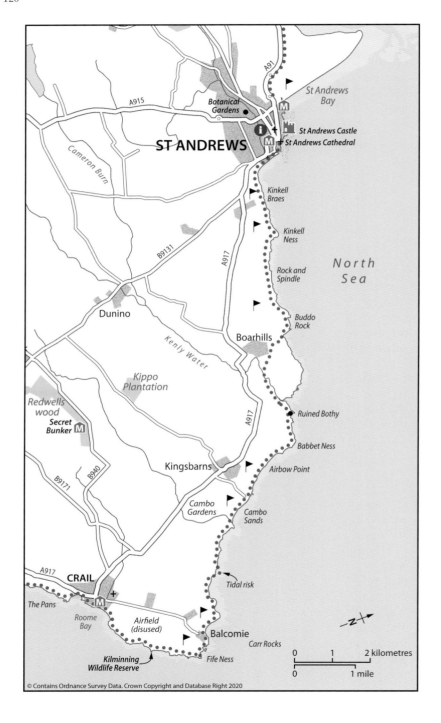

© Contains Ordnance Survey Data. Crown Copyright and Database Right 2020

VII
Crail to St Andrews
(The Cold Coast)

O.S. 59 / 371

If you have stayed in Crail overnight perhaps you can ask for a Crail *capon* for breakfast—a haddock done local fashion. I doubt if you will be fulfilling the recommendations of an old guide (in its chapter on 'Swimming, Sailing and Drowning') which points out, 'It is one of Crail's recreative laws which, it is hoped, will be honourably observed, that Roome Bay is available for gentlemen only up till eight o'clock in the morning'.

It is essential to be away as early as possible, for today's walk (at least 13 miles through to St Andrews) can take a good eight hours and is by far the roughest and toughest day, many grades up on anything else. For much of it there is no easy escape and no refreshments or other facilities, so carry adequate supplies, especially drinks (streams, running off farmland as they do, should not be used). If in doubt there are escapes inland to the Crail-St Andrews road (A917) at Cambo, Kingsbarns and Boarhills, 5, 6 and 9 miles on from Crail (hourly bus service) and one could plan to do this anyway if a long, hard, challenging day does not appeal. Parts of the route can be muddy or jungly, there are frequent switchbacks, a couple of places are impassible at full tide and there is a danger of landslips. Walkers, perforce, must be prepared to boulder-hop, scramble and slither. You have been warned! Kept for a good, dry day, this 'Cold Coast' ('Golf Coast'), offers open, spacious, atmospheric, wild coastal walking quite unlike anywhere else on the coast and should be relished for those qualities.

Head off along the Nethergate or, from Marketgate take Kirk Wynd, opposite the church, which leads down to the east end of the Nethergate. Take the left fork in the path almost at once, down and up and round below the houses, a flowery walk with good views. At the start, over on the right, is a white sixteenth-century doocot ('The Pepper Pot'). Unusually, there is no string course. An erratic boulder on a reef offshore is the Mermaid's Cradle. When I was a boy and these bungalows were built we thought it amusing when one was bought by a retired doctor who named it Kilmeny. The house next door was also taken by a retired doctor. He called it Kilmore. Past the houses the path swings back to the coast. A last view of Crail shows how good a sea mark the doocot makes.

Walk straight through the unexpected Sauchope Links Caravan Park. This lies on the site of a golf course that pre-dated Balcomie, Crail's original links. The caravan site is on the lower raised beach level (about 5000 years old) while Crail largely occupies a higher raised beach some 15,000 years old. Continue on by the path which keeps close to the shore be-low the obvious raised beach slope. (The sea is cutting into it now too.) The lumpy rock on the point ahead is Kilminning Castle, a natural sandstone outcrop, and is at the start of the Kilminning Coast Nature Reserve (SWT). The bay beyond has a boulder beach and ends at a wartime machine gun post. Cattle graze this end of the reserve to reduce the rank growth and encourage a greater biodiversity. Above is the old airfield of HMS *Jackdaw* with its decaying buildings. The Fleet Air Arm station was built on the site of the village called Goats. German bombers raided the airfield: Crail received several hits and there were fatalities in St Andrews. The path rises towards a big shed and leaves the reserve though we are still in an SSSI (Site of Special Scientific Interest). Suddenly the mast and coastguard buildings on the Ness lie just ahead.

The 1998 creation of the Craighead Links (golf course) lies to the left, behind a good example of new dry-stane dyking. We drop down and along to 'the end of Fife', **Fife Ness**, passing under the more imposing buildings of the coastguard station and colourful houses, then wend up to squeeze by the thrust of grey rock below the unspectacular light. There's a Fife Bird Club hide and another old machine gun post built by Polish forces in 1941. Here we have the last view back to the Forth estuary and the now distant marks of the Isle of May, Bass Rock and North Berwick Law. The grey rocks below are strangely worn, and a contrast to the jagged basalt strata running out just round the corner when we pass under the light. The Forth has expanded from the half-mile wide river at Kincardine; the distance from here over the open sea to Dunbar is 19 miles.

For most walkers the main interest will be the stiff-winged fulmars which skim the cliff thermals all along the coast. They arrive early in the year and leave at summer's end, staying out at sea over the winter. They only start breeding when seven

At Fife Ness.

years old and only lay a single egg, yet the twentieth century saw their breeding range expand from a few remote islands off NW Scotland to encircle the British Isles. Gannets, blazing white with black wing tips, the Concordes of the seas, are also likely to be seen, the Bass Rock being one of the world's biggest breeding sites. The Bass is such an historic site that the bird is actually named after it: *Morus bassana*. Watching gannets diving can seriously delay walkers! Eiders bob and croon among the rocks. The Forth Estuary has over 20% of the UK's population of these crooners.

The Carr Rocks and Fife Ness generally have seen a score of ships lost (listed in B. Baird's *Shipwrecks of the Forth*), three being paddle steamers: *Windsor Castle* 1844, *Queen* 1857 and *Commodore* 1859. Another paddle steamer took the name *Commodore* and was also wrecked, at St Andrews, in 1896.

The small tarred road is joined and curves round past several caravans facing what was once Fife Ness harbour. This was mostly natural and occupied an exposed and dangerous site—yet it was here Mary of Guise landed before going on to St Andrews to marry James V. At one time stone was exported to Rotterdam. If you look carefully on the north shore below the cottage you may see the circle of an inter-tidal spring, then a more obvious larger stone circle in the rocks, which gives rise to all manner of speculative ideas, but the true explanation is that it is an archaeological site to do with the notorious Carr Rocks. Further out lies the Bell Rock which, in 1799 alone,

Fife Ness.

sank 70 ships, and when Robert Stevenson managed to erect a light there (a saga worth pursuing), he was asked to tackle the Carr Rocks, the reef off Fife Ness.

The old harbour was restored for landing the stone, which was cut with this circle as the template for the dovetailed stones. A tower was planned and a coffer dam had to be created on every visit to the reefs, so in 1813, the first year, only 41 hours of labour was possible, in 1814 only 53 and in 1815 most of the work was destroyed by the sea. It took two more years to complete only to be utterly destroyed again. They gave up. A cage-like marker on iron legs was built on the base in steel, easy enough to replace when need be. Now a single pole carries a radar reflector. There's an explanation board at the site. Older folk can recall a red lightship which now sits in Dundee harbour.

Keep round the sea's edge to another display board at the site of a one-time tidal mill (we passed one at Burntisland). Return, briefly, to the road. The oddity of a village pump stands by the road, the only indication of a hamlet at Fife Ness long ago. Turn off to pass between golf course and the tidal pool. White markers indicate the edge of the Crail Golfing Society's course.

The Crail Golfing Society was founded in 1786 and is the seventh oldest golf club in the world. The markers show the crest of the Crail 'ship' topped by eighteenth-century golf sticks. The attractive course was first laid out by Old Tom Morris.

Round a first point, on the left of the track, stands a cave. Tradition has it as Constantine's Cave, where the king was killed, c.874, at the hands of raiding Danes. Sandy Balcomie Bay now sweeps ahead. Walking is safer on the sands (even there I once had a golf ball roll at my feet). The obvious building on the dunes has roundels above the walled-up seaward side showing its earlier use as a lifeboat station: a crown over 1884 on one, the other a lifeboat above the letters RNLBI. At the end of the sand is the Blue Stone, the other erratic paired in legend with the one at the gates of Crail church. Inland we can just glimpse Balcomie Castle where Mary of Guise had B&B in 1538. Now it is part of a farm.

There are two golf courses now at Balcomie, so they extend well round the bay with white markers throughout. Keep to

The Balcomie coast.

the banks or the shore beyond to swing round to a stile below the headland (the official path goes high up just to descend again). Cliffs (fulmars overhead) fall sheer to the sea with no real alternative (except waiting) if the tide is right up (has to be a *very* high tide). A secondary prow also entails a tidal passage before one can gain the edge of cultivation—and yet another golf course, the highly-praised Kingsbarns links, with red markers along its edge.

You can walk on the shore or along the edge of fields/golf course, or a FCP inland loop, to reach the bridges over the **Cambo Burn**. The larger bridge with the decorative letter K has been made to blend with the 'Japanese' footbridge seen upstream. Seaward is a footbridge for golfers who play along the sea's margin to the exposed 15th hole out on the point.

The Cambo Burn comes down through attractive woodlands and it is worth a diversion, both for itself and to visit the walled garden. Walk up beside the burn (masses of snowdrops, daffodils and hyacinths in season) past the graceful curved footbridge and then cross at a second. The path heads on passing left of the walled garden to reach the A917, but turn right to follow the wall round, right, to the garden entrance (open 10.00-dusk). Interesting at any season. From the parkland beyond you can see Cambo House and, across the park, a fancy doocot (tower with finials), the sort of thing that followed the beehive/lectern types so often

Cambo Gardens.

seen. In places there are families of pigs—practical pigs for rooting up the ivy to allow snowdrops to prosper. The Stable Block has been turned into a visitor centre with plants for sale and an unusual café. The Cambo name comes from a grant by William the Lion to the de Cambhou family. An Erskine bought the estate in 1668 and it has remained in their family ever since. The lush setting is quite a surprise on the Cold Coast. Return to the sea by keeping to the path down the right/south bank. The FCP has an alternative here of going up the glen a bit from the K bridge and then heading inland round the golf course, but most walkers I'm sure will want to keep to the coast.

From the bridge over the Cambo Burn follow the track on, circle the trees (where there is a 'Restrooms' building) then follow the dunes along the edge of this undulating golf course, crossing one burn, to come out at a car park/ picnic area (with seasonal toilets), served by a road down from Kingsbarns. At most tides it is as easy to walk along the warm-coloured sands. The road leads up to the A917 at Kingsbarns, an old hamlet where the king did once collect and store grain for use at Crail or Falkland. Remains of a harbour can be seen once past the toilet block. We continue walking along the edge of the golf course, the last green edged with an enormous bunker. At a wall running down to the sea there's a warning that the going ahead can be 'hazardous/tidal' but this should only seriously affect passage on rare occasions. Hereon, walk either on dunes or on the sands, all a bit 'up to you'. There's one larger beach, then a couple of smaller strands, the first ending at a very visible coal seam and, past the second, another ruined salmon bothy. There's a track up to the main road where we keep along a wall to reach the barrier of the Kenly Water. Kenly is from the Gaelic *cean liath*, grey head.

The Kenly Water could be paddled at low tide but the going beyond is neither interesting nor easy enough to make this worthwhile, so the best route (and the FCP) turns inland for a pleasant enough diversion. In winter and spring the woods are massed with snowdrops, anemones, primroses and wild hyacinths in turn. You may spot a dipper, and wrens are noisily present.

Just before reaching cottages the FCP drops, right, to continue alongside the Kenly Water, a woody dell that seems quite surprising on this wild coast. A side stream comes in at a ruined mill, and there are lots of hartstongue ferns. Eventually cross a sturdy footbridge and walk up by the attractive Burnside farmhouse.

Turn left and follow the road up a brae which brings Boarhills into view. When the road swings left take the dirt track off right (FCP sign) to follow field edges along to massive green barns. Turn right round the barns (note the lectern-type doocot) and then break off, first right, on a green track which leads over naked fields back to the shore. A gate/stile gives access to the curve of bay with the strange feature of the **Buddo Rock** prominent. On clear days the Angus hills can be seen and towns as far up the coast as Arbroath.

The FCP avoids Boarhills which is a pity for it is a charming, flowery hamlet and a diversion adds little in distance or time. You rejoin the FCP at the green barns.

The main bulk of the Buddo Rock, a pink sandstone, has a cap across to a beaked pillar and, unexpectedly, there is a split up the rock so it can be climbed—adventurously—with the help of some steps and holds carved out.

There are some shallow caves in the cliff beyond Buddo Rock. Follow the path over the wall to angle up to the top of the bank (where we first meet the St Andrews Bay golf course complex), the first of many ups and downs, which should be followed, to avoid salt marshes or ragged shoreline. We still have bracken, brambles and thorns to contend with. This is one of the most noteworthy sections of the FCP, terrain more

High seas off Kenly.

Buddo Rock.

usual on the West Coast. The path drops down to the shore at another dell.

Kittock's Den only has a small stream, and is bridged (*kittock* is a giddy lassie!). The prow beyond is the site of a prehistoric fort. Kittock's Den comes down from Boarhills and the jungly scrub is a haven for winter migrants blown in off the North Sea. I've seen redwing and fieldfare passing like blowing leaves in November. The very lucky might see waxwing in winter after an easterly gale.

The small bay ends with a wall/stile at shore level and an, at present, unmade higher bypass. The path turns up steeply back to golf course level with clubhouse, hotel, a pond etc. inland, and follows along the boundary wall. A gully is spanned by a mini-Bailey bridge and then the path angles down to go through a tunnel in the blackthorn. Ahead is the striking feature of the Rock and Spindle.

You have to take to the shore and may be delayed by a high tide. A handhold is provided at an awkward corner (below high tide mark). The path along the green slopes thereafter has laid slabs. At low tide the shore is pleasanter till past the Rock and Spindle. Keeping along the slope ends with a vigorous down and up which leads to easier going with St Andrews and its towers and spires in full view.

The base of the **Rock and Spindle** has a circle of basalt rays ('like the rays of a daisy') and little imagination is needed to

The Rock and Spindle.

envisage a bubble of lava exploding to create it. The whole is a volcanic plug; all that is left of a weathered eruption of lava that burst through the sandstone millennia ago. The slender pinnacle can be climbed, an easy but exposed task, but that is a game best left to climbers. Tracks coming down to the coast here led to a now vanished harbour, and local farmers also took up seaweed to manure their fields.

The steps have taken us up onto the Kinkell Braes. Nearing the caravan parks, a descending path (steps) goes along above the Maiden Rock, another isolated sandstone feature sometimes the playground of rock climbers. Its first mention in this context is by Harold Raeburn (1902); he found 'the complete traverse of the *arête* a nice little climb'. A path leads down to the shore, but it is really easier just to keep along the braes. The rocks beyond the Maiden are full of *encrinites*, the fossil remains of cylinder-shaped sea creatures which show clearly as white circles in the darker matrix. Kinkell is *ceann coille*, head of the wood.

The higher path along to the Abbeyfield Leisure caravan site soon drops down as well, the two re-uniting before the lower St Andrews Holiday Park caravans. The path past the caravan site has been moved back as erosion has nibbled away at the cliff. There's a real feeling of achievement on descending

The Maiden Rock with St Andrews beyond.

to the East Sands, a bay curving round to the harbour with its long sheltering arm. The cathedral ruins dominate the view. On the left there are inscribed granite semi-circles (like seats) which bear the words of a poem by Jacob Polley (T.S. Eliot Poetry Prize winner in 2016). 'East Sands, Salt Print' was inspired by St Andrews' early connection with photography. A tarred footway runs along past the East Sands Leisure Centre, the Scottish Ocean Institute (St Andrews University; the first ever marine laboratory), Sailing Club (in the old lifeboat building; there's a good snackbar) and play area. In 1864 a severe storm washed up a sea worm 55 metres (180ft.) long on the East Sands. A footbridge crosses the lifting gates of the inner harbour which now is a small marina, rather than home for a one-time fishing fleet which operated in these dangerous waters. It has a sluice to let water out to clear sand from the outer harbour.

Turn right along by the flats, whose level roofs make them the most inept restoration seen on our walk. The harbour arm is long and, as most do, gives a worthwhile view from its far end. On Sunday morning students still walk the pier wearing traditional red gowns. The harbour arm was built in the winter of 1655 by women from the Netherlands. The stones were pillaged from the wrecked cathedral. From the side of the flats walk up under the old signal station to the site of the Church of St Mary on the Rock, a twelfth-century foundation (see the descriptive notice board). Little is visible, and the site was only discovered when constructing a coastal battery in 1860. Two cannons face out to sea and there's a view along the cliffs to the castle. The cliff top walk is a delight, and you'll be eye-to-eye probably with the nesting fulmars, 'planing the thermals with insolent skill'. The first fulmars (once a rare northern bird) first nested here in 1947 in their gradual colonisation right round the British coast.

The path forks: the right fork leads along the cliffs, past the Castle and University Museum (MUSA) along the Scores to Murray Park (left) which has many accommodation options, the left fork comes out to the end of North Street, and on round outside the cathedral, becomes South Street. Market Street lies between, reached from either. North Street is largely taken up with university buildings, South Street and Market Street are more commercial. Other B & Bs tend to be on the outskirts; there are several hundred options—unless there's a major golf

St Andrews Harbour.

St Rule's Tower and Cathedral ruins.

tournament in progress! The Tourist Information Centre is in the middle of Market Street (no. 70), and it would be worth a visit now to pick up a town map and anything else of local interest. Accommodation can be booked there too.

Fife is full of interesting names. In the East Neuk you will find Lingo, Lumbo, Blebo, Tosh, Kippo, Swinkie, Ribbonfield, Ragfield, Bonerbo, Bonnytown and Balhouffie—for starters.

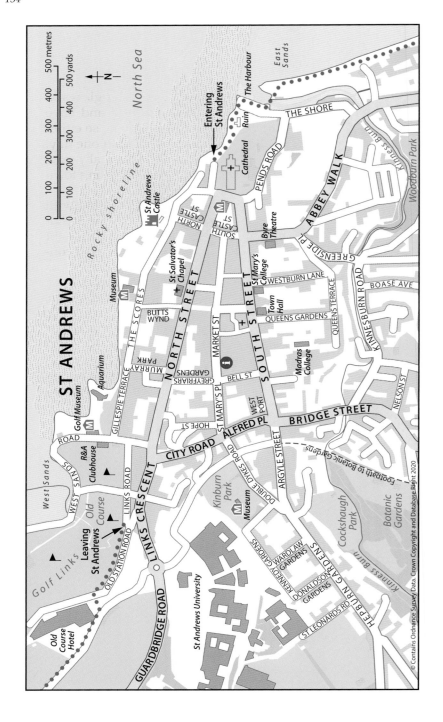

VIII
Exploring St Andrews

This exploration of St Andrews is described as a single walk-about, but you would need to be strong-legged and have ' 'satiable curiosity' to fit in everything mentioned, so either be selective or spread the walking over more than one day. If a visit was not made previously, do call on the centrally-sited Tourist Information Centre (70 Market Street) to obtain a town map and the current information on *What's On*.

St Andrews originally had the name Kilrymont, but with the legendary arrival of the apostle's relics it became St Andrews. The relics were supposedly brought by St Rule (St Regulus), but he was a Celtic missionary with no local connection. A Northumbrian connection may be more likely, as Hexham was known to have housed relics of the saint and these may have been bought or brought on to St Andrews. David I granted the town's charter *c*.1144. Like many old towns it was once walled; unlike most, one of the ports (entrances) has survived, and we'll start our perambulation at this, the **West Port**.

The gateway was reconstructed in 1589. In 1650 Charles II was presented with the key of the city here. Now it demands a one-way traffic system. Head off along South Street. The Gifford tome has comments on almost every house; we'll, perforce, be more selective. On the right there is an older house with a forestair and the oval logo of the St Andrews Preservation Trust, which was founded in 1937 to rescue and restore some of the classic domestic architecture. St Andrews too was lucky that a retired military type from India became provost in the 1840s, and went about rebuilding the civic spirit and its historic buildings and monuments. There's a mural monument to Sir Hugh Playfair in the cathedral cemetery and a Playfair Aisle in the historic Town Kirk. The minister then was another Playfair; his monument is an elaborate marble pulpit. The initials of previous ministers who had been Moderators of the Church of Scotland decorated this pulpit, including Playfair's, but no room was left for subsequent initials and, strangely, the kirk has not produced a Moderator since!

On the right, look down Louden's Close, typical of the old runrig system. Walking on, still on the right one comes

John Knox preaching in St Andrews (display in the Castle).

on a small ruin, which is all that remains of the Black-friars Monastery with the imposing Madras College behind, across the lawns. The ruin is the apse of the 1525 chapel. The monastery was smashed following John Knox's 1559 St Andrews sermon. (Knox had earlier been imprisoned in the castle and spent some time as a galley slave in France.) As in most places in the town there are interpretive display boards. The 'suave Jacobean manor' was built by William Burn and opened in 1834, founded by Dr Andrew Bell, a local lad, son of a hairdresser, who worked in the USA, was ordained and went as a missionary to India where he worked out his Madras monitorial system. The school was co-educational, unusual for the time. The fine façade hid somewhat Spartan realities; one rector wrote of donning two sets of woollen underwear in October and keeping them on till April. Some classes started at 06.00. Having outgrown the premises they are moving to a new campus on the edge of town.

Cross the street to go through a pend (passage) to cobbled Burgher Close, a typical courtyard. When you come out, turn left where a plaque commemorates John Adamson, pioneer photographer, who took the first ever calotype photo in 1841. We then come on the **Town Kirk**, Holy Trinity, the roof covered in Caithness slabs, the chancel floor Iona marble and with a blaze of stained glass. Only the tower is old (*c*.1410). Entering, the many-pillared arches recall the great mosque at Cordoba. Gifford calls the church 'a dictionary of architectural quotations'. The tower was often used for locking up sinful women, and cutty stools (repentance seats) and the branks point to intolerant times.

The branks were an iron head-fitting frame with a bar into the mouth to make speech impossible. Archbishop Sharp had the branks on one Isobel Lindsay to stop her heckling during his sermons. He was to be murdered on Magus Moor above St Andrews not long after. Hackston of Rathillet, one of the ringleaders of the assassination, was judicially butchered and parts of his body hung up in various towns as a warning. A huge near-contemporary marble monument shows the hated archbishop's end. In 1849 when his tomb was opened it only contained a broken coffin and no sign of human remains. This was where John Knox preached his rabble-rousing sermon in 1559 which led to the direct destruction of much church property. Old Tom Morris, the Royal and Ancient's first professional golfer, has a memorial, among many others.

Diagonally across from the church is the baronial pile of the 1858 town hall, which replaced the Market Street tolbooth. There are associated mementos on display. Provosts are listed back to the twelfth century. Royal Burghs only lost their unique character in 1975 government reorganisation. The clock hangs over the street, a Polish memorial and provost lamps on the side street.

Beyond the church is the Tudor-style building of J. & G. Innes (stationers/booksellers). The site was the home of Bailie Bell, the father of Madras College's founder, who had a mechanical flair and worked with an Alexander Wilson on a system of type founding that made their names. Wilson was associated with a Philadelphia foundry and cast the first-ever $ sign (in 1797).

Turn left along Church Street, which was originally Kirk Wynd before gentrification, to reach Market Street, the old heart of the town where cobbled crosses indicate the past sites of mercat cross and tolbooth. There is a Saturday street market, and the Lammas Fair in early August is the oldest surviving mediaeval fair in Scotland, dating back to 1153 at least. Five fairs once attracted pilgrims and traders from all over Europe. Latterly the Lammas Fair was largely a fee-ing fair (for signing on farm workers) and now is simply a funfair. The fountain is a memorial to novelist George Whyte-Melville who died in a hunting accident. The hapless Chastelard (caught in Mary Queen of Scots' bedroom—twice) was executed here in 1563 and so was the Bohemian reformer, Paul Craw, who was slowly burned to death in 1433, a brass ball forced into his mouth to prevent him speaking to the crowd.

Cross Market Street onto College Street to reach North Street. **St Salvator's Chapel** tower dominates the scene.

Between North Street and the sea the area is largely university buildings. Bishop Wardlaw was the recognised
founder of higher studies in St Andrews in 1410, based on
Orleans. A papal bull two years later confirmed what was
to be Scotland's first university (in Britain only Oxford and
Cambridge are older). St Salvator's College was founded by
Bishop Kennedy in 1450. The Kate Kennedy Procession each
April recalls some of this history, Kate's part being played
by a 'beardless *bejant*', as first year male students are called.

The tower at first had no steeple, and in 1546 the Protestants who had seized the castle were bombarded by French
cannon from the top of the tower. In front of the pend through
the foot of the tower the initials PH on the cobbles indicates
where Patrick Hamilton, a young, well-connected and likeable
student, was burned in 1528—the deed taking several hours.
Walk through the pend to the Jacobean-style quadrangle and
the entrance to the church is on the right, the interior glori-
ously rich and colourful. Bishop Kennedy's tomb and John

Kate Kennedy Parade: Kate and Bishop Wardlaw.

Knox's pulpit are preserved and there are monuments to old boy Andrew Lang, the Borders poet, historian and folklorist. One keen golfer who studied at St Andrews was the Marquis of Montrose. Among the Rectors of the University have been Andrew Carnegie, Rudyard Kipling and James Barrie—and the Norwegian explorer Fridtjof Nansen.

Return to Market Street and, near the Tourist Office, go through Crails Lane to South Street, then cross over to the archway entrance to **St Mary's College's** attractive quadrangle. The holm oak dates to 1728, but centuries earlier is the propped-up thorn by the bell tower, planted, tradition claims, by the ubiquitous Mary Queen of Scots. Archbishop Beaton founded the college in 1539. The buildings on the east side include the James VI library, gifted in 1612. In 1645 the Scottish Estates met here, and the room has been Parliament Hall ever since. The sundial dates to 1664. The statue is of Bishop Wardlaw. The French influence is due to French workers being borrowed from the construction of the palace at Falkland.

Continue eastwards along South Street, lined with sturdy old town houses of character. Janetta's is a justly famous ice cream parlour: over 30 flavours to choose from. South Court Pend leads to a courtyard, lit in season by a flowering cherry tree. A plaque commemorates Professor J D Forbes, one of the early alpinists and the scientist who astonished contemporaries by showing that glaciers were 'rivers of ice'. Abbey Street, next along, right, has the Byre Theatre where the original tiny (73 seats) theatre was created in a byre (cowshed) in 1933. It has been rebuilt twice since. Continuing along South Street, the cathedral ruins are framed at the end of the street with, left, the leaning corner tower of the Roundel and, right, Queen Mary's House. The gateway beyond is the Pends (an old priory entrance) and leads to the harbour. As you swing left, another cobbled cross before the Deans Court gateway marks where the 80-year-old Walter Myln, apprehended at Dysart, burned at the stake in 1558 on the orders of Archbishop Hamilton, himself to be executed in 1571 for being involved in the murder of Darnley. Henry Forrest, another student, also suffered here in 1533, for the crime of possessing a *New Testament* in English. Cross the road to enter the **Cathedral** grounds.

The building itself is a 'rent skeleton' (Ruskin) but, at over 100m. long, it still indicates past glory. Display boards describe the scene. The museum in the old refurbished priory

St Andrews Cathedral.

buildings should not be missed, the early sarcophagus panels being one of Scotland's most treasured and breathtakingly beautiful antiquities. There are many assembled gravestones; one, on a windowsill, shows death as a skeleton stabbing his victim in the back. In the entrance is a slab with several 'Green Men' worked into the patterning. A token purchased in the museum will give access to the 33m. high, square, St Rule's Tower, the finest viewpoint in St Andrews. Within the east side choir there's a mural slab showing a skeleton lying in a hammock. Facing it is a monument to Dr Thomas Chalmers, who was Professor of Divinity among all his other activities. A walk round the wall of the graveyard will produce everything from full-rigged ships to golfers like Tom Morris, father and son, and Willie Auchterlonie, the last local to win the Open— in 1893. Tom Morris, senior, won the second-ever Open in 1861 and then again in 1862, 1864 and 1867. His 17-year-old son won it in 1868, 1869, 1870 (no championship in 1871) and 1872, the first ever four-in-a-row. Young Tom died aged 24. James Anderson, of a golf-ball-making local family, won three in a row, 1877–1879. A feature film, *Tommy's Honour*, tells the story of father and son. Golf has to be added to Town and Gown as the St Andrews triumvirate.

The grave of young Tom Morris.

The Cathedral had an unhappy history. The west front was wrecked in a storm, Edward I of England stripped the lead off the roof, and fifty years later it was gutted by fire and took seven years to restore. One bishop, captured by English pirates, refused to be ransomed in order not to sidetrack funds. At the time of Bishop Wardlaw the south transept was blown down. In 1472 it became the metropolitan see, and for a century nothing fell down or went up in flames. In 1559, however, the Reformation instigated the 'burning of images and mass-books and breaking of altars', and the Cathedral became a quarry for building stone for the town. The Cathedral was originally consecrated by Bishop Lamberton, staunch ally of Robert the Bruce (who was present), and for crowning Bruce at Scone, Edward I had the bishop put in chains.

From the Cathedral head along North Street. Left is the St Andrews Preservation Trust Museum, with displays of grocer's and chemist's shops from more recent, more peaceful, times. Not for long though; turn right into North Castle Street (ex-Castle Wynd) and head for the **Castle** visible ahead. Cobbled initials this time point to where George Wishart was burned in 1546 while Cardinal Beaton looked on from a castle window. Not long after a small gang of

Protestants managed to seize the Castle—and the cardinal's body was hung out of the same window. Henry VIII backed the Protestants, who held out for a year. The Castle was 'dang doon' several times before that, though. Little of the structure survives (the harbour was repaired by pillaging its stone) but the Visitor Centre has a fascinating audio-visual display telling the story of the fortress. Two features are notable however: in the Sea Tower is the Bottle Dungeon, and one can explore a mine and counter mine. The former is carved out of solid rock, bottle-shaped, the only access via a rope lowered down the 'neck'. No one ever escaped its dark, dank depths, and the sea was there for taking the victims' bodies. (The sea has now taken the whole east range with its Great Hall.) In a 1546 siege the Earl of Arran began to mine towards the castle walls to lay explosive charges, quite an undertaking as the passage was big enough for ponies to pack off the rock. The tunnel sloped to pass under the defensive ditch, and a chamber was prepared under the walls, only for a desperately-searching counter mine to break

St Andrews Castle from St Rule's Tower.

Early golf-ball maker (St Andrews Golf Museum).

through and spoil the attempt. Going through these tunnels is a memorable experience.

The street leading along westwards from the castle is The Scores (ex Swallowgait), at the far end of which are several other features, but they, I'm sure, would need another day after this marathon walkabout. They deserve a mention however. The big attraction is the Wardlaw Museum (MUSA: the University museum), full of historic treasures and fascinations Fulmars nest on the cliffs and the Aquarium lies below, its largest 'pool' the old Step Rock tidal swimming pool, much used in hardier times. Witch Hill with the Martyrs' Monument (some restorations in 2013) and trim bandstand is also the old Bow Butts, where archery was practised. In 1457 James II tried to ban golf (and football) as archery was being neglected. Both James VI and his mother were great at the 'gowf'. The British Golf Museum is bunkered into the hill, a high-tech, fascinating place with old mementos and audio-visual displays. You can see historic replays, brush up on history, follow the careers of the greats and lots more. There's a café. The Royal and Ancient Golf Club is just across the road and the historic Old Course (and others) lead away along the West Sands to the Eden estuary. The ladies' putting green is nicknamed The Himalayas. The West Sands give several kilometres of walking, usually with a snell wind. The setting was used for the opening sequence in the film *Chariots of Fire*. Do walk along

The scree in St Andrews Botanic Gardens.

the sands, perhaps to round off the day. Out Head, the far end, is a nature reserve, and from the high point there's a view to the dunes stretching away by Tentsmuir to the Tay Estuary.

In 1991 the St Andrews Museum opened in a castellated mansion in Kinburn Park, telling the story of the town in a lively style (café). In the gardens is the Sikorski memorial, commemorating the wartime leader of the Polish forces. The museum is on Doubledykes Road, the continuation westwards of Market Street, and nearby, too, is the site of the impressive Botanic Gardens, a 10-minute walk on a path from the car parking area. The Kinness Burn 18-acre site is attractive at all times, and there are large glasshouse collections. The Cacti House has over 250 species, there are collections of alpines, rhododendrons, primulas and aquatic plants, all in a magnificent tree-rich setting. (All Scotland's native trees are represented.) There is also a Tropical Butterfly House, café and, often, plants for sale.

In medieval times pilgrims from all over England and the continent *walked* all the way to St Andrews. This rather puts our brief expedition into perspective, but we become, having shared the physical and mental stimulus of exploring the Fife coast to St Andrews, part of the long tradition. Perhaps, next time, you can reach St Andrews by the inland Fife Pilgrim Way, with its starting point Culross or North Queensferry.

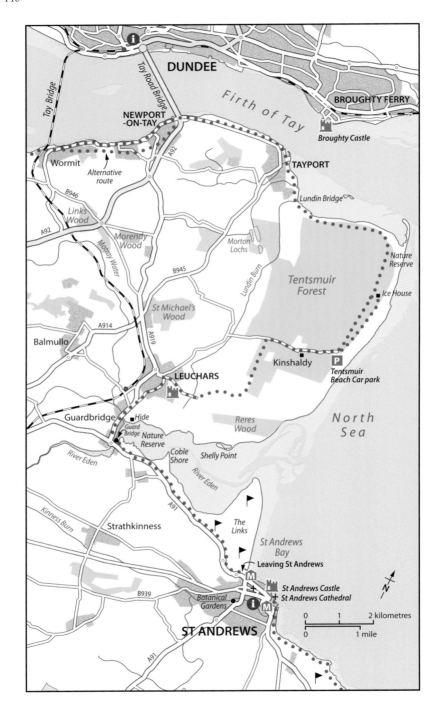

IX
By Tentsmuir to Newport

O.S. 59 / 371

The only option for the 4 miles of FCP from St Andrews to Guardbridge, the lowest bridging point on the River Eden, is to follow the Millennium Cycle Way which runs close—all too close—beside the busy A91.

The Open comes to St Andrews every few years. Winners, working backwards over the last few, have been Zach Johnson (2015), Louis Oosthuizen (2010), Tiger Woods (2005 and 2000), John Daly (1995), Nick Faldo (1990), Seve Ballesteros (1984), Jack Nicklaus (1978 and 1970).

The Society of St Andrews Golfers was formed in 1754 and became the game's regulatory body. The 'Royal' was added to the title when William IV became patron. The clubhouse was built in 1854. There are several courses on these links: the Old Course (so old it can't be dated), the New Course (1895), the Jubilee Course (Queen Victoria's, 1897), the Eden Course (1914), the Strathtyrum (1993, pronounced Strath-tye-rum) and the Balgove beginners' course (9-holes, 1972).

Starting at the R&A Golf Club (Golf Place) and heading inland, we pick up the FCP to turn first right, The Links, where houses overlook the 18th hole of the Old Course (which

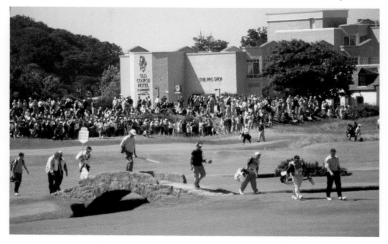

The Millennium Open at St Andrews.

makes it Millionaires' Row). The iconic Swilcan Bridge lies off right and then we pass the 17th hole. (Interestingly, the Old Course is public land so anyone can play on it.) We turn off on reaching the Old Course Hotel (FCP signs) and, leaving the entrance, turn right (FCP sign) along a road which ends at the A91.

Just before the main road, turn off right on the Cycle Way/ FCP path which will be our route through to Guardbridge. As far as the courses continue there are trees between us and the A91—no doubt to protect the motorist from flying golf balls. The route is tarmac and these 4 miles must be the least walker-friendly part of the FCP. (There's a bus every 15 minutes to Guardbridge!) The route eventually just becomes A91 pavement, and the senses are given maximum punishment from speeding traffic. Surely a line could be taken further from the A91? There's a footpath heading down to the local nature reserve at the Coble Shore point. On the far side is Coble House Point, and Sand Ford Head between suggests this waist in the estuary might once have been a ford.

We continue along the A91 with what was a paper mill at **Guardbridge** dominating, and a big quarry behind halving hapless Lucklaw Hill. We soon come on an old toll house, recognised, as most are, by windows giving clear views both ways, in order not to miss any traffic. There's also one of east Fife's attractive cast iron milestones (St Andrews 3). Shortly, on the other side of the road, at the Strathkinnes junction, is the

Guard Bridge.

The Guardbridge Hotel a few years ago.

Hungry Horse café. On a bit, turn off right, taking an old piece of road signposted for the Guardbridge Hotel (now called the Guardbridge Inn), which has picnic tables and a pleasing view of the inner estuary. If imbibing, do go inside to see a collection of old prints and paintings of the area. One shows a steam train on the bridge. A notice on the wall caught my fancy: 'Be warned that tickling and groping is an offence under section 27 of the Salmon and Freshwater Fisheries Act 1927'. The hotel/inn no longer has its outside walls covered in butterflies.

The Eden Estuary has now narrowed to a wide tidal river, 22 miles from its source in the Lomond Hills and its course through the rich farmland heart of Fife. This lowest bridging point has been well used over the centuries. Beside it, the main road goes over a triple-arched concrete bridge, typical of its 1938 period, while downstream are the stumpy piers of the 1852 Fife Coast Railway (North British), which followed round from Leuchars Junction to St Andrews, Crail and the other East Neuk towns to Leven and Thornton Junction. The line was axed by Beeching in the 1960s. What a tourist lure it could have become with steam trains running on it now. The old bridge was built by Bishop Wardlaw early in the fifteenth century, which makes it one of the oldest bridges in Scotland as well as one of the most pleasing. In 1685 repairs were made from the revenues of vacant stipends and the bridge was referred to as Gair Bridge. Guard is just a corruption of this. There are bold cutwaters and six arches, the most easterly being smaller, and three refuges (recesses for pedestrians) on each parapet, which may be of later date. Panels bear the arms and initials of Archbishop James Beaton.

Once over the River Eden turn right (on the A919 now) into the village of Guardbridge. There's a few surprising buildings in brick, including a one-time church (over left), then the impressive old facade of the 1899 Guard Bridge Cooperative Society—note the date on a fancy gully box and the clasped hands motif.

Look out for signs for the Eden Estuary Centre, an attractive birdwatching hide (with disabled access, toilet) looking over the upper estuary, which should not be missed. The whole Eden Estuary is a local Nature Reserve and SSSI of international importance for its birdlife, the relatively pollution-free waters ensuring plenty of mussels, cockles, snails, worms and algae to feed the thousands of wildfowl and waders. Shelduck and red-breasted mergansers are common, and you could see long-tailed duck, eider, scaup, common and velvet scoter, oyster-catcher, ringed and grey plover, bar-tailed godwit, black-tailed godwit, redshank, curlew, lapwing, golden plover, knot and sanderling according to season, as well as peregrine, osprey, stonechat and garden birds. Four species of geese over-winter. There's a useful leaflet available at the centre and recent sightings are marked on a blackboard.

Near the path to the hide the pediment of the now gone 1920 Memorial Institute marks the World War I list of those killed—33 from this hamlet. There is also a memorial for a L/Cpl. David Finlay VC (1915). Back on the road, we now reach what looks like an industrial site. The site was originally that of the Seggie Distillery (belonging to the Haig family, 1810) and there was also a pulp-mill and brickworks. When these failed, the Guardbridge Paper Company was established in the distillery building in 1873, so there was well over a century of papermaking at Guardbridge. It closed in 2008. The site is being developed as the Eden Campus of St Andrews University. Already in operation is a biomass plant which supplies the university (5 miles away) with hot water/heating. The site is also that of the renowned Eden Mill Brewery and Distillery (shop, tours, tastings etc). All this is reclaimed land, where there was once a port for Cupar and the Howe of Fife. Cross the road and continue.

We then pass over another old bridge, the Inner Bridge or Motray Bridge, only replaced by the new road in 1938. The

Motray Water was essential for the paper-mill which, in 1967 for instance, used 20 million gallons a week (more than the town of St Andrews!). The estuary was necessary for exporting whisky, bone meal, wool, paper and agricultural produce, and the three piers could cope with 32 vessels which seems incredible now. Something like 200 vessels came to grief on this part of the coast, so the coming of the railway was welcomed. The paper-mill was bombed on a sneak low-level raid during World War II, but no damage was done.

Continue on by a play area and houses to reach the Balmullo junction with the A919. Continue along the A919 briefly, turning off right, for the minor road into **Leuchars**. The road runs through a mix of military (right) and housing (left). For many decades this was RAF Leuchars but it closed in 2015 and the skies fell silent. The Army now have the site but its future is not certain (the RAF might return). In World War II it was an RAF Leuchars fighter which first engaged with the enemy.

A bend suddenly brings Leuchars Church, up on its knoll, into view, a startling change, for the village retains a douce, almost mediaeval atmosphere. We turn right onto Wessex Road, then onto Earlshall Road, but first have a good look at the church—and perambulate the site if the gates are chained up. There is no drinking water between here and Tayport (10 miles ahead), so stock up if need be.

Leuchars Church – a Romanesque treasure.

Leuchars and Dalmeny (above Queensferry) are the two finest Romanesque churches in Scotland, with magnificent arcading giving the prize to Leuchars. The chancel and apse are twelfth-century, and the apse roof was replaced by the octagonal bell tower in the sixteenth century, with a lead weathercock. Corbel heads above the upper arches are of animals, real or imagined, and human and grotesque faces. A papal bull mentions the church in 1187 but it was (re)-dedicated in 1244 with the name of St Athernase. One minister, a noted preacher, Alexander Henderson, was Moderator of the 1638 Assembly in Glasgow which abolished episcopacy.

Earlshall Road passes the primary school (on the left), and continues on to Earlshall Castle. The garden has famous topiary work (the trees are a bit like chessmen) and the potting shed roof has finials of romping monkeys along its ridge. There's an old sundial and a rather superior doocot dated 1599. Earlshall's gardens are occasionally open to the public.

The Bruce family of Earlshall probably built the castle in the days of James IV. The second laird lived through the reigns of James IV, James V, Mary and James VI. He fought at Flodden and died with James VI the acknowledged heir to the united kingdoms. His tombstone is in Leuchars Church, dated 1584, declaring Sir William had died in his 98th year. *Mors omnium est finis*. A later laird was an ardent ally of Claverhouse. He butchered Richard Cameron, the hardline Covenanter, at Aird's Moss and captured Hackston, one of the assassins of Archbishop Sharp, who was then barbarously executed in Edinburgh. After James VII went into exile he became a Whig. His son left only daughters and Earlshall went to the Hendersons of Fordell by marriage, after which it went through many owners. Mary Queen of Scots stayed at Earlshall, of course. (All monarchs in those days moved round their realms: which meant free D, B&B and allowed them to keep an eye on their nobles.)

Robert Mackenzie, a bleach merchant from Dundee, bought the castle in 1890. His peers thought him daft, but he knew exactly what he wanted, and he engaged the young Lorimer to restore the building we have today. In 1926 he sold the estate to Sir Michael Nairn, the Kirkcaldy linoleum tycoon, who gave it to his daughter as a wedding present.

Past the castle we skirt the old airfield perimeter briefly, passing Comerton Farm. The track wiggles on by, or in, odd stretches of trees. When the track turns hard right at the end

Kinshaldy road in Tentsmuir Forest.

of a plantation and 200 yards on, left, the FCP goes through two pedestrian gates and along a fence-enclosed walkway (to protect walkers from cattle!). After 150 yards turn right, following a field edge, to the boggy open woodland. There are duckboards. Lots of duckboards. Eventually turn left through a long waymarked grassy glade with scattered woodland and, at the far end, a bridge leads into **Tentsmuir Forest** proper, a huge planting over a flat landscape that still has some unusual features.

This is an area of delightful wildness, rich in birds, insects and flowers. There is no shortage of skylarks here—or on many days along the coast. Look out for gaudy cinnabar moth caterpillars crowding on ragwort. Last time here I came up to within fifteen yards of a fox and spent twenty minutes watching it hunt through the long grass, unaware of my presence. When it did scent me it was off in a flash. One Tentsmuir snag—be warned—in high summer there can be a horrible plague of flies.

Head on along the forestry track to reach the small tarmac Leuchars-Tentsmuir Beach road. Turn right. Shortly after, the Polish Camp road goes off on the left and is so-named for Polish forces who were stationed here in World War II to build the sea defences we will be seeing. A fine beech avenue leads on to Kinshaldy.

Kinshaldy Riding Stables lie just off to the right, and ponies will be seen in the few fields islanded in the oceanic spread of Tentsmuir Forest. There's a pay-barrier (for cars!) thereafter, and, after half a mile, the large Tentsmuir Beach carpark, where there are picnic tables, toilets (in summer), display boards, big children's play area, summer café and access to the vast sands.

Tentsmuir Forest goes back to 1922, planting on what was basically salt marshes at the NE corner of Fife. The Stuart kings once hunted bears in its wilds, and shipwrecked sailors and all manner of broken men hid in its fastness. Salmon fishing eventually brought some respectability to the coast. The NE corner, dunes, the Tayport heath and Morton Loch, form today's Tentsmuir National Nature Reserve. The trees are mostly mature Scots or Corsican pine. (An area of birch lies seaward of the icehouse.) Tentsmuir was the third NNR set up in the UK in 1954.

Mesolithic people roamed the sea's edge 8,000 years ago. A dug-out canoe has been found, and heaps of shells from eating places which were then by the sea, now by the road from Leuchard to Tayport.

Tentsmuir has very diverse bird life; besides herons, moorhens and gulls here, there are wrens, green and great spotted woodpeckers, sparrow hawks, curlews and warblers. Other species abound: colourful snails, rabbits galore, foxes, roe deer and red squirrels. Go quietly and you may see some of these. Bat boxes have encouraged three species to live in the forest (natterers occupy the ice house). Grey and common seals haul out on the remoter sandbanks. Butterflies include the common blue. Husky dogs are occasionally met in winter, for teams race in Scotland, but on wheels rather than sledge runners.

The FCP simply follows a major forest track (from the inland far corner of the parking area) which gives an unvarying tramp of little character, so it is much more rewarding to either walk the sands as far as the Nature Reserve boundary or take a path, the Ice House Trail (red markers) which runs nearer the forest edge up to the Ice House. Access is from the seaward far edge of the parking area.

A salmon bothy is passed, later a World War Two pillbox and, finally, right, through a gate, a stylish timber-built shelter/ interpretation centre which has information on every aspect of Tentsmuir. Don't miss it. Seawards, you can see the World War II observation post and the most extensive sands at low tide. In the far north east seals like to haul out. Don't wander into the reserve, however. Heading inland, the Ice House is reached beside the big track, the main interest of the walk. The trail we have followed returns to the Tentsmuir carpark by the main track, but there are still options for continuing on our way to Tayport.

The 1852 Ice House is one of those half-sunken, grassed-over, insulated buildings where salmon in this case could be kept fresh in summer. Ice was carted/shipped from the Highlands in winter months to estates all over Fife and the Lowlands (fridges came in somewhat later!). Remember the ice house at Culross? Walking on along the main track, after a junction for Morton Loch, is the Salmon Stone, like an elongated milestone, a 1794 march (boundary) marker between two salmon fisheries. A bit further on a path heads off right. Take this to the edge of the Nature Reserve where there are information boards (they are everywhere with any interest), here describing the slacks: wet hollows with their own flora that attract many insects (like the vivid burnet moth). A wind pump helps to keep the area flooded. The grazing cattle help

The Ice House.

to prevent the dunes being taken over by seedling pines, an ongoing concern for scientists. Back in the 1960s there was a debate that they should be cleared as they were man-introduced or left as, these being trees, seeding was natural. (I once camped for a week with a school party at Morton Loch farm, our remit the removal of all the seedlings from one half of a specific study length of dunes.)

Rather than return to the big track, follow a forest-edge path which soon brings one to Tentsmuir Point where we turn from sea to estuary. We look across to the sands of Buddon Ness (which hide Carnoustie) and up the Arbroath coastline. Wartime concrete blocks, an anti-invasion device, are everywhere now. At one time all stood at the high tide mark, even those well inland. Tentsmuir gains ground eastwards by about five yards a year! It is quite a thought that some of the grains of sand could have come from the slopes of Ben Alder or Ben Lui or Schiehallion.

The big track keeps well in from the shore hereafter but the forest edge can still be followed. Either way the last stretch is another slice of Nature Reserve with specific characteristics, the Tayport Heath. At the forest entrance are various information boards, picnic tables and direction/distance posts, one for Morton Loch–a famous birdwatching venue with hides. Heading on we pass an area which can be covered by a really high tide.

There are machine gun posts up on the bank and a last scatter of anti-invasion blocks; along the beach here many are

Tayport Harbour.

Bell Rock Tavern gable.

half-buried in the sand, as erosion is nibbling into the forest edge, a contrast to earlier. Offshore names appeal: Lucky Scalp, Tony Scalp, White Scalp, Tom's Hole, Snook Head…

Lundin Bridge ends the Tentsmuir interest; ahead **Tayport** (once Ferryport-on-Craig) strings round to its harbours, where estuary narrows to become river, once a vital ferry site. Turn right at a display board (eider mosaic) and wander round the seaward edge of the large green areas, cross a bridge and skirt the seaward edge of a caravan park to reach the East Common. Keep to the Promenade till it swings inland where a path, right, runs along the back of the houses and pops out at the yacht-busy harbour/marina. (In really rough weather follow the promenade road to its end and turn right onto Harbour Road.) Offshore lies a pile lighthouse, built in 1848 when the Tay was busy with whaling vessels. It looks a bit like 'a dalek on stilts'.

Tayport Harbour as we see it dates to 1847, and was constructed as the Fife terminal for the Edinburgh and Northern Railway ferry, one imitating the Burntisland-Leith 'floating railway'. The older village of Ferryport-on-Craig took on new life as a result. The rail bridge has rather eclipsed Tayport (while Newport, Woodhaven and Wormit prospered) but a ferry over to Broughty Ferry operated till 1939. Historically this was the crossing taken by drovers heading south. Broughty Castle indicates its strategic importance; the castle on this side has disappeared, the only hint in the name Castle Street.

Walk round the harbour. Inland lie the Bell Rock Tavern and community-run Harbour Tearoom. Broad Street runs up to the town centre, shops and an old kirkyard with beautiful nautical picturings. Tayport sprawls with many wynds and secretive corners and plenty of architectural interest, but exploring is probably not practical now. A display board points out that President Ulysses S. Grant crossed the Tay by ferry in 1877 and made a point of studying Bouch's new (not yet disastrous) rail bridge.

Continue along to the West Shore where there's another harbour/slip and turn left through a court of attractive modern houses built to blend with more traditional styles. A red gravel footway leads on up deviously to reach a road and houses. Turn right and, soon after, right again, down a steep hill. After 100 yards turn off, left, onto the start of an easy-angled path that points to once being a railway (from Dundee to Tayport). Two lighthouses stand on the shore, built by Robert Stevenson. Originally identical, the eastern abandoned, the west rebuilt and painted white, a notable sea mark. The route rises steadily through a pleasant tree avenue, then open farmland. The B946 is reached. Dundee now fills the view, some of the tower blocks looking as high as the Law.

The Cycle Way/FCP now runs along parallel with, and just below, the B946, with only one parking loop interruption.

West Light, Tayport.

Tay Road Bridge.

Ignore cycle signs, and 100 yards on (beyond the colourful sculptures opposite) cross at a FCP sign and up to the **Tay Bridge** carpark (toilet, café kiosk). If crossing the bridge a pedestrian/cyclists' track lies in the middle of the bridge, between the vehicle lanes, an odd feeling after the Forth Road Bridge.

The road bridge was opened by the Queen Mother in 1966 and must be regarded as functional rather than fascinating. (north east Fife's water main comes over it in a 24-inch pipeline.) There's a dramatic obelisk marking the roundabout at the south end and the bridge's lines are not unattractive. Walking across is a good way to finish. In the centre of the walkway the tiles are laid out in the pattern of the knight's move in chess: the architect was a champion player.

Two miles upstream is the railway bridge (slightly larger) which crosses to Wormit, while between the two bridges the south shore is continuously built-up: Newport-onTay, Woodhaven, Wormit, with Pluck the Crow Point central.

Dundee, Scotland's historic fourth city, deserves some notes. If not now, at sometime do walk across the bridge, a memorable experience. Crowded between the volcanic plug

Tay Railway Bridge: from Wormit over to Dundee.

of the Law and the Tay (120 miles from its source), the old town has been transformed many times, but much of interest lies within short walking distance of the road bridge.

Nearing the Dundee shore the waterfront is dominated by the prow-like thrust of the V&A building and, behind it, Discovery Point, where the masts of Captain Scott's *RRS Discovery* (built in Dundee) will already have caught the eye. Next door is the Olympia Leisure Centre (big swimming pool, climbing wall etc) and nearby the oldest warship afloat, the frigate *Unicorn*. In the city centre, (Albert Square) is the striking McManus Galleries with strong representation of Victorian/ twentieth-century British art, McTaggart and Patrick, besides specialities on pre-history, wildlife and the Tay Bridge disaster. The award-winning Dundee Contemporary Arts complex is very popular, as is the Perth Rep Theatre. The Law (174m/571 feet) is a great viewpoint, and on Balgay Hill the Mills Observatory is open to the public. The Howff, an historic graveyard in the town centre, has typical craft symbol stones. The Tourist Information Centre is found in City Square.

Dundee, lying on the east coast route to Aberdeen, has had a stormy history even by Scottish standards and has always had a certain pioneering spirit. It was once Britain's chief whaling port, and a hub of the textile industry. The old saying of 'Jute, Jam and Journalism' was certainly true. A Mrs Keillor invented marmalade and D C Thomson remains firmly in the city—producers of everything from the *Beano* and *Dandy* to *The Scots Magazine* (which dates back to 1739). The city has always had strong medical connections with both research and production, which continue to this day. Dundee is also very much a student centre with 39,000 students, including the Universities of Dundee and Abertay and the Duncan of Jordanstone College of Art.

162

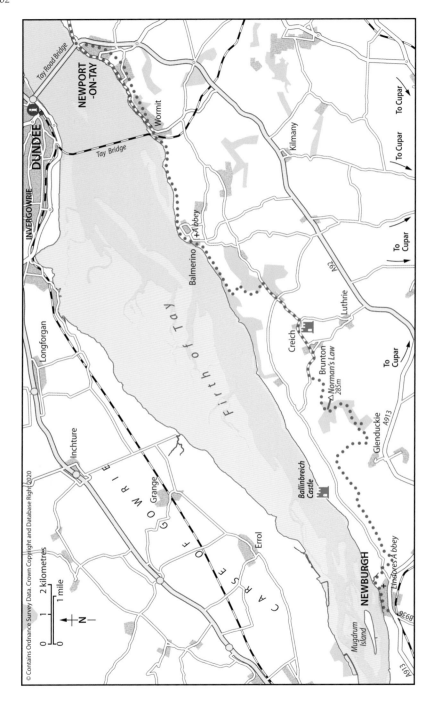

X
Newport to Newburgh
O.S. 59 / 371, 370

From the Tay Bridge carpark the FCP heads through the
pedestrian passage under the bridge approach and descends
steps to regain the B946 (Tay Street) which is followed for
almost 5 miles to Wormit, urban walking along the seafront
all the way. There is a more rural and peaceful option, so read
both and decide which to follow. Both have merits. They are
described in turn.

The houses overlooking the Tay are often opulent as the
setting appealed to the well-off industrialists of Dundee,
who could afford to live away from the smoke and grime of
their creations. There is a certain charm in how they seem to
tumble down the hillsides—and what fine views they have.
The V & A Dundee looks very ship-like from along here but,
strangely, is being launched bows-first.

The first notable object as we walk the seafront can't be
missed: a particularly well-preserved and painted Victorian
cast-iron fountain right beside the road. Do look up at the
canopy *from inside.* The war memorial follows and then the

The fountain on the seafront of Wormit.

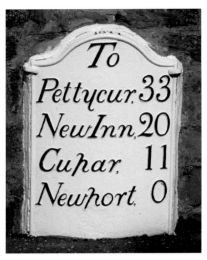

Newport milestone.

road dips, as the High Street, with its shops and services. The B946 road forks. The church on the apex has had a change of use. Keep right, downwards (the one-way system is for cars!) where there is Kitschnbake Café and a pub and then the Boat Bay Restaurant (windows right over the river) which occupies part of the building associated with the important Newport Ferry. On the wall there's a milestone rather stating the obvious: Newport 0 (and Pettycur 33). Pettycur-Newport was the main coaching road north across Fife.

The first steamship ferry came in 1821 and paddle steamers would operate for a century. The last crossing came in the evening of 18 August 1966, following the opening of the road bridge by the Queen Mother in the morning. (I knew the ferry well; on one occasion, cycling home from Aberdeen on the last day of the school holiday—I'd a girlfriend in Aberdeen—I was so broke I had to scrounge the necessary sixpenny fare off some kind person.)

There's a bit of a brae up thereafter and, without much urban change, we are walking through Woodhaven, which at one time had a ferry competing with Newport (now the site of Wormit Boating Club). We continue on into Wormit. Riverside Road seems to draw the rail bridge closer. Before we come to it, some of its history.

The Tay Bridge is always thought of in connection with the disaster of 1879 when Sir Thomas Bouch's original single-track bridge collapsed during a violent storm, taking a train with it and killing 75 people. A bridge of over two miles across the Tay estuary was an ambitious project and Bouch was perhaps unlucky to be a pioneer. The cause is still debated, but basically the bridge was too frail–which is why the Forth Bridge was made so immensely strong. The present double-track bridge was begun in 1882 (Engineers, W. H. Barlow; contractor, W. Arrol). It recycled some of the original girders and was completed in 1887, when it was the longest rail bridge in the world (and is still the longest in Britain). The foundations of the first bridge lie along the seaward side of the new like gigantic stepping stones.

The second option from the Road Bridge carpark is now outlined.

At the edge of the carpark towards the bridge you'll see a Scotways sign: 'Nature trail. Public path to Birkhill Avenue, Wormit. Follow green signs.' As we pass under the bridge, why not go up and walk out on it a bit just for the experience, and the view. From the west side of the underpass the steps down (FCP) have been described, what you might call 'the low road'. To misquote the song: 'Oh, you'll take the High road and I'll take the Low road, and I'll be in Wormit before you' would probably be accurate.

We turn left, inland, to walk up and round between houses, dip to cross Craighead Crescent, and take a gravel path on. At a sort of junction turn left onto what is Norwood, a street of sturdy Victorian villas. At a junction (Station Brae, which leads down to the High Street) turn right, then first left, to follow Linden Avenue. At the next road, go straight over and up to follow what was once a railway line. There's a bit of parkland then the path dips to what is the busy Cupar Road. (There's a traditional milestone indicating Pettycur 32, Newport 1.) Turn left, uphill, pass an entrance to Tayfield, and a bit on, turn right along Kirk Road: a very rural feel. As the road bends, cross to take a path/steps down a wooded area and, almost surprisingly, come on the only really open area with good views. (The Low Road gives the better views.)

This was the site of Newport West Railway Station on the Dundee to Tayport line which opened a year after the rail bridge in 1879 but then would close again almost at once (for eight years) with the tragedy of the rail bridge collapse. There's a description board which has some words by the poet of the silvery Tay, William Topaz McGonagall. The service

A Wormit villa, now Post Office and shop.

ended in 1969 when the Road Bridge opened but the houses of Newport, Woodhaven and Wormit were already in place so from here on the old line could become a footpath—a nice balance to our walking up out of Tayport on the same service line.

Some garages are passed, then there's a sharp turn left. On, cross what is Castle Brae to a carpark (sports centre, left) and exit under a small old bridge. The long, gentle descent indicates the old railway line. There's a down and up to cross Flass Road and another lengthy stretch of old line. When walking the line ends, we drop down right, on a steeper path to what is really the end of this High Route. There's probably the best possible view of the Rail Bridge as we leave the line. Turn right down Birkhill Avenue to the main road (B946), which is the earlier, lower, choice of route, and continue along Wormit.

The rural walk thereafter to Newburgh is 15 miles, a long stint, half over hills, so might be more pleasurable if split into two parts. (I've done this by using a Cupar taxi to/from pretty Brunton.)

There is a FCP sign indicating to leave the B946 down Bay Road but if café, shops, pub appeal they lie a few minutes further along. Wormit's claim to fame is being the first place in Scotland to be connected to a domestic electricity supply

early in the twentieth century. One walks under the big
red brick arch of the railway.
Note a post-box with VR
(Victoria Regina), quite a
rarity. There's a long carpark
above the pebbly beach and
at the far end three granite
slabs remember the names
of those who perished in
the 1879 bridge disaster
when the central high spans
collapsed under the stress
of storm. Fifty-eight names
are listed.

A hard surface path leads
to the end of the beach where
there's a seal to sit on and
relax before heading up on a
path or track which rises and

Wormit post-box.

then undulates along the hillside, periodically giving grand
views to the bridge. There's another seal seat at a larger open
space, an area where Himalayan balsam riots, a den (steps) and,
eventually an ash-edged wood for a longer cared-for woodland
with a variety of deciduous trees. That ends with a longer flight
of steps down to sea level. The FCP heads between houses and
shore, the start of Balmerino, locally (and anciently) Balmernie.

On the Wormit-Balmerino path.

Just about every home in the village is an old building which has been converted, with respect, so the result is charming. This first group of buildings was once a fish-processing plant and the white cottages, soon after, were fishing bothies and, on a bit, mill and farm buildings have been reborn. The large erratic on the shore is known as Samson's Stone. Soon after turning up, inland (a last seal seat), FCP signs point to a path off right but first do explore the Abbey and top end of the village. Not a few houses have 'No entry to Abbey' on their entrances and the NTS site is simply reached through a gap, unsigned. There is not much to see as the original Cistercian 1229 foundation was burned, like so many, during Henry VIII's 'Rough Wooing' (1547) and then, in 1559, 'decommissioned' following John Knox passing on his way from Lindores to St Andrews. The vaulted sacristy and chapter house still stand, though rather propped up—as is the famous old Spanish chestnut tree. Legend has it being planted by Queen Ermengarde, widow of William the Lion who was buried here in 1233, but core sampling points to a bit over 400 years, the time of James VI. James Elphinstone, secretary to James VI, was created Lord Balmerino. He and his heir were both executed and the sixth Lord Balmerino lost his head on Tower Hill in 1746 for having backed the disastrous Bonnie Prince Charlie.

Balmerino Abbey ruins and the ancient Spanish chestnut.

The village ends with a formal memorial square, a very practical war memorial, dating from 1948. An oak tree stands in the middle of the green, statues depict the four seasons and the Doric portico dates to c. 1812 and came from Birkhill—a mansion further along the coast—which the FCP will skirt. Head down again. The road, off right, heads up to war memorial and graveyard, with some interesting stones, one showing a shepherd's crook.

The FCP path leads down to and along the edge of the shore initially before heading up to wend along through a delectable wood, the best such on the whole FCP. Nearing the end (Birkhill grounds) it turns up inland, and then up a field edge and *up* will be the word until past Norman's Law and the FCP highest point. Turn right onto a track and then left at a fork to join the Birkhill drive which climbs steadily to a junction with a minor road (Muir Dens), and so back to tarmac walking. Turn right. A house on the right is called Corbiehill (Crowhill) and the crossroads we go over is Hazelton Walls. The whole area has what an old book called 'a congeries of hills' and the mix of knobbly hills, woods, fields and secretive hamlets like Brunton is pleasing to the eye. We turn right to pass the stark remains of Creich Castle.

The castle was a Liddles property till they were forfeited for treason and it was bought by the Beatons in 1502. One Elizabeth Beaton was a cousin of the ill-fated Cardinal—and mistress of James V. Mary Beaton was one of Mary Queen of Scots 'Four Maries'. The ruined church is next passed. Creich was the birthplace of Alexander Henderson (1583-1646), foremost statesman of his time, who was minister at Leuchars Church which we noted. Our route passes above Brunton and at a junction, turn right.

Heading on, Pittachope Farm appears. Beyond it, left, is a layby with a display board with Norman's Law information. (The one thing I can't discover: who was Norman?) The FCP heads off 100 yards beyond on a track which wends upwards steadily and then breaks off, right, on a grassy track that runs through trees to more or less circumnavigate the Law (good FCP signing). Before heading off on the green track, walk on for one minute on the farm track to a rise from which there is a pleasing landscape view.

Keep an eye open for a single stile which gives the access for Norman's Law, a summit not to be missed. A clear path crosses a field, goes over a wall and twists up to the summit

Norman's Law.

with twin white trig point and dark view indicator pedestal that have dominated the view of late. Norman's Law is 285m (935ft). What a summit panorama! The Lomonds lie in mirror-image of what is seen from the Binn; there's a whole horizon range of Highland hills, from Ben Lomond to Macdui, Schiehallion pokes its symmetrical cone into view, while, downwards, the Tay sprawls from the mudflats off Newburgh to the Tay railway bridge and Dundee. Largo Law stands clear. In the same direction the nearer hill with a narrow tower on top is Mount Hill, the tower (1826) a monument to Sir John Hope, one of the distinguished commanders in the Peninsular War. The Law cairn may be ancient, the summit area being a Pictish fort. Norman's Law has the feel of a real hill (it is only 17 feet lower than Largo Law) and never disappoints. I've seen it in both stark January and early summer with a tapestry of yellow rape fields and dark woods, and best, watched a glorious sunset set the upstream river aflame.

Rejoin the forest track and continue the woodland circuiting of the hill. At one point we are on the highest point of the whole Fife 'Coastal' Path. The path drops steadily, steepens and comes out of the trees with fields sloping up on the right (the gate tells us we've been in the Aytonhill Forestry Estate). We pass a track up to Ayton Hill, then come to an easy-to-miss fork back on the right which has the names October Cottage and Briardene indicated. Take this. Opposite a third cottage a footpath heads along and then down a long field

The view from Norman's Law.

edge to a barn. A farm track then leads on to a depressingly low point where we fork back right to regain nearly all the height we've lost. At least the walking on is pleasant as we next circuit Glenduckie Hill, another with Iron Age summit vestiges. A sign notes Melgers Woodland Estates. There's a dip and we swing up left to a big gate with a pedestrian gate bypass. The track becomes a path, there are younger trees on the right (sycamores) and after losing some height the path turns sharply right to descend and exit the trees to follow a fields' edge progression through a series of gates. We are still looking south down an open valley towards Dunbog and other humpy hills of Fife's volcanic past. Eventually however we wander up a field edge to gain a view, a fine view, of the River Tay. (Remember the River Tay? The Fife 'Coastal' Path?)

The descent starts at a large red gate (FCP signs), down a broad green track which we leave when it ends at another red gate to wander along through a narrow belt of pines, the cultivated slopes falling away below to the river. When we leave the trees the path/track continues at a gentle angle on an ancient pathway. It ends cutting through gorse and more woodland edging. (A word of warning: this is all well-grazed land and there are ticks, so have a body check before bedding.) The steep final descent starts past the first obvious way 'down' but is clearly signposted, drops through fields (orchard on left) and comes to a substantial track. Turn right and come to a tarmac road, turning left along it for Newburgh. The town sign is ahead but the FCP makes one of its illogical choices to break off, right, at a burn, pass a sturdy wooden bridge and follow round the banks of the Tay, Newburgh perched inland, to eventually exit at the other end of the town in a carpark to declare its official ending. Why does the FCP declare its starting and finishing places being Kincardine and Newburgh and then ignore them completely?

Logically one would just carry on up the road, passing the town sign and this could well be done as, just after, are two attractions, from which one can carry on into town, or back-track for the attractive-enough Tayside walk. Most welcome will be the Lindores Abbey Distillery, which opened in 2017, in doing so restarting a brewing/distilling history which had been lost for 500 years, when the Abbey closed down. It is a popular venue, open for visits, and meals and refreshments. The McKenzie Smith family bought the abbey and farmland in 1913, and, today, have created a pleasant combination of distillery and a verdant, peaceful place to rest. The ruins of Lindores Abbey make a pleasant setting but the stonework, such as remains, is lost below an avalanche of ivy. The Abbey was founded in 1178 by the Earl of Huntingdon, brother of William the Lion, and, as a spin-off, came the 'new' burgh. Abbey and town had many royal connections (the Earl of Rothesay burned the Abbey in 1402) and in 1543 the monks were expelled briefly. Knox wrote it was 'well reformed' in 1559. The last abbot died in 1596. The reason it became such a ruin was the pillaging of stone rather than the Reformation. A curious fact: because of the harsh climate the monks had the Pope's blessing to wear bonnets. The Abbey bell was carried off to St Giles in Edinburgh. At one time the Abbey was sup-posedly infested by adders. There are none today. James IV ordered one of the monks to make Aqua Vitae in 1494 – the first record of distilling. The monks were also famous fruit growers, and orchards today are likely a direct descendant from the abbey years. Wandering round the Abbey there's the moving sight of the two very small stone coffins, for the infant sons of the founder. A large stone coffin was for the notorious, intriguing 'Black Douglas' who was banished to the Abbey and, surprisingly, died in his bed.

Having no doubt enjoyed refreshments at the distillery and relaxed in the Abbey we should backtrack to complete the FCP loop along by the river. (If pressed, one can walk on and there are bus stops on joining the main road, and the Buttercup Café

The still house in the Lindores Abbey Distillery.

at the corner garage.) And, on leaving the Abbey site, look up to where the FCP comes down off the hills. Ploughed onto the slope is the figure of a bear holding a staff – symbol of the Earl of Warwick (his crest also appears on a building on the High Street). The connection appears to be that the first Abbot of Lindores came from a cadet branch of that family, but this hillside marking is not ancient like English figures on chalk hills. FCP walkers are welcome to pitch a tent at the distillery; just ask.

Our path follows the banks of the Tay with a knuckling of hills on the far side. Himalayan balsam soon gives way to the sweep of reedbeds, once important for thatching. We join townlands again at the Newburgh Sailing Club but keep on by the riverside, passing a series of piers in whose lee are anchored some of the old salmon-fishing cobbles with their upturned bows. Lamprey are also present in the Tay. There's a sculpture of salmon in an arc of green set back from the river. The Tay reedbeds are the largest in Britain. One fifth of UK's bearded tits occur on the Tay. A tagged marsh harrier from here was tracked across Europe and down to wintering grounds in West Africa.

Where we finally leave the riverside Mugdrum Island is just that, and not reedbeds or sandbanks. What fascinating names the banks have: Wonder Bank, Reckitlady Bank, Kerewhip Bank, The Turk, Peesweep Bank, Sure as Death Bank, Eppie's

Macduff's Cross above Newburgh.

Taes Bank, Carthagena Bank. Landward names too abound in the curious, cheery names like Robin's Brae, Washer Willy's, Gettaway, Pickletillem, Glenduckie, Blinkbonny; murkier names like Lockmaloney, The Clink, Dark Law, Foodie, Gallow Hill; and try getting a tongue round Mountquhanie or Cunnoquhie.

All this sweep of park-like green is land restored by the local Community Trust from what was an intensely industrialised area of mills and factories and a harbour exporting grain or swapping cargoes from seagoing vessels onto lighters to be taken up to Perth. Linen once dominated but there was a linoleum works too, the only one to challenge Kirkcaldy's dominance. It closed in 1980 following a disastrous fire. (I've sharp memories of these works standing right over the river. I'd a school party canoeing past under the walls when a pipe suddenly jetted out a cascade of boiling water which, luckily, landed on the tail of my canoe. A second earlier would have been 'interesting', the lads thought.)

The riverside path curves inwards and the FCP heads left on a gravel road, then right at a tarred road to enter a final park area. (Before doing so walk on one minute and look back towards a slip to see a brilliant *coup d'oeil* of an eagle.) Follow up paths, left, to finally come on the Kincardine-style Fife Coastal Path archway; the end of the journey.

Do walk down to the town, however. Bowling green and war memorial are passed and from the Victory fountain there's a good view of the attractive High Street, an early nineteenth-century unity unspoiled by post-war horrors. The pastel shades remind of Irish villages. The town was only ever this one street, with garden strips below or above (many with orchards) and reflects a certain prosperity. James VI in 1592 made it a Royal Burgh, a status confirmed in 1631 by Charles I. I've a record of the town in 1882. It had a Post Office, savings bank, Commercial Bank, seven insurance agencies, four hotels, waterworks, a gas company, cemetery, public library, reading room, coffee house, two bowling clubs, a gardening society, a natural history and archaeological society, lawn tennis club and a young men's religious institute, and a Parish Church, Free Church, UP Church, Baptist Church and Evangelical Union.

The Parish Church was a William Burns 1833 gothic creation. The cemetery, perforce, was outwith the town. I've mentioned how superstitious fishermen could be but others were little better. Even after suicides were allowed to be buried in consecrated ground, in Newburgh the coffin of a suicide was lifted over the wall, rather than taken in the gate, the fear being the next child to be christened would, in later life, commit suicide. Newport, at the end of the seventeenth century, was the scene of a fatal duel fought between Sir James Macgill of Lindores and Sir Robert Balfour of Denmiln.

Heading down from the top of the town, on the left, is the unpretentious frontage of the 1894 Laing Museum. This fills

Newburgh High Street.

Sunset on the Tay.

an impressively spacious hall and includes a recreation of the study of historian Alexander Laing who gave his unusual collection (and 3000 antiquarian books) to the town. There is much on the local heritage, with a family history resource.

An attractive modern square stands next to the museum, where the very first church was erected. (On, you'll see a one-time church is now a house.) Down, on the other side of the High Street, the tall building with clock and spire was the 1808 town house. On that side the Bear Tavern has the Warwick crest. Across from there is a 1758 decorative lintel with a sailing ship, the symbols of navigation (sextant and compass), presumably from a prosperous merchant who, nevertheless, had the motto 'omnis vanitas'. High Street becomes Cupar Road at the 1887 Livingstone Fountain. If the Abbey and distillery were not visited on arrival, they are reached in a few minutes from this low end of the town. There are shops, pubs, café etc., and bus-stops at regular intervals.

As we started with the River Forth, perhaps the last word should be about the River Tay which we have followed from being a wide estuary to this waisting of its waters. The 120-mile River Tay pours more water into the sea than any other river in Britain. Strictly speaking it only becomes the River Tay on leaving Loch Tay at Kenmore, earlier being the Dochart (from Killin back to Crianlarich) and the Fillan (to near Tyndrum), but most allow its main source/origin is on the slopes of Beinn Laoigh (Lui), birthing the Cononish Water—a grand genesis for a grand river. Not a tame river. There are records of bridges being swept away in Perth in 1210 and 1648 and in 1814 a superstorm saw the river seven metres above the norm which caused havoc everywhere. From the first day of 1740 the River Tay was frozen solid for six weeks.

In the sixties I took a school party exploring Perth harbour. A dredger was kept busy on the river, this work allowing small ships to use the harbour. The material taken from the river bed was separated into many grades of gravel and sand, a very 'green' piece of commercial exploitation. I recall one boy picking up a small stone and saying in awed tones, 'This chuckie could hae come aw the wey frae Ben Lui', a grand concept for the grand river. And not many miles south from Beinn Laoigh is Ben Lomond, on whose slopes begin the waters of the River Forth, the river where our walk of the Fife Coastal Path began. The FCP has been given the status of being a one of Scotland's Great Trails. You now know why.

Appendix 1
The Binn to Kinghorn

From the end of the Burntisland esplanade turn under the railway (Lochies Road), cross the A921 to go along Greenmount Road South. At a T-junction turn right onto what is Kirkbank Road and follow this to its end where a footpath heads up through woodland. This comes out on the B923 Kirkcaldy Road. Turn right. Cross at the Golf Clubhouse entry and on left take a steep path up through the woods. (Green sign: Public Paths to the Binn.) The woods are a mass of snowdrops through February into March. After some steps and a safety rail there's a cross path of sorts.

Ahead, lies the Binn village ruins (historical description board), right is our continuation after ascending the Binn (large flat boulder), for which climb we turn left and then leave the woods to go up a field edge, over a wall, and a final crest with wind-tortured thorn trees. In a gap in the trees look out

On the Binn, distant North Berwick Law to the right.

for a crag with big-ringed netting on it. This is recycled World
War II anti-submarine netting. They, and concrete barriers,
were to prevent rockfalls or landslips endangering houses
below. Now the slope is naturally overgrown with shrubs
and trees. The summit has a bench and view indicator. We
are at 193m (632ft).

No need to describe the view, then, but there have been
changes. You can pick out the coastal pallet manufactory, the
swimming pool complex and, right below us, Burntisland's
Primary School. Just visible, regimented rows of houses mark
the site of the once huge aluminium works. The sea view
sweeps from Bass Rock to the three Bridges—a fantastic mix
and match from here. Inland, the tall Craigkelly transmission
mast is now near. Right of it are the Lomond hills: the Bishop, and the West and East Paps, separated by a wide saddle.
Kirkcaldy is clear, and Largo Law, and it is a sobering/en-
couraging thought that we are walking to pass the furthest
point visible. (We'll eventually look *back* on the Bass Rock.)
The crumbly rock of the Binn does yield a rich flora.

Heading down (as we came up), from the wall crossing you
will see, ahead, two small wind turbines edging a large grassy
area, probably being grazed by horses (and loved by hares).
This is part of the Whinnyhill landfill site. Under the grass are
decades of waste from the aluminium works, now restored
on the surface, but the underground 'leachate' will take many
years to clear—hence the two wind generators which make
the site self-sustainable. You can read more shortly. 'Alcan',
as locals still call it, operated from 1917 to 2002.

Nearing the bottom of the field you may spot ruins among
the trees (off left) and at the cross paths you can read all about
the Binn village, another industrial giant which had its time
and then disappeared. From here, under the Forth, and much
of the Lothians, the land is honeycombed with the workings
of the one-time vital shale oil industry. At one time the Binn
had twelve rows of back-to-back cottages, a school for over 200
children, a mission hall and shop. All gone. The site closed in
1905 but for some decades people came over from Edinburgh
on the steamer *William Muir* to holiday at the village.

The regular incline of the fenced-off path/track/path we
now follow points to it once being a mineral line (shale heading to Kinghorn), now all part of the Whinnyhill site, above
and below. A cycle track joins and there's a wide grassy viewpoint area with picnic tables and excellent information boards

Binn village as it used to be.

describing these Binn industries. We come out to the B923 once more. Turn left, pass the Whinnyhill site entrance, then left onto a farm track indicated as a Public Path to Kinghorn Loch and Redbraes. We follow the track all the way up and round to Craigencalt Farm, but heading off right are many woodland paths, which are a must in snowdrop time, leading to Kinghorn Loch. There is, first, a track off left for the Toll Bridge; worth a ten-minute circuit to find the troll and a bench at a viewpoint above. There's a bird hide at the loch. Swans nest, as do great crested grebes and rails. Kingfishers are seen. The loch is the winter base for Kinghorn Coastal Rowing Club (and their skiff, *Yolande*). Carp fishing is popular. Rafts of barley straw prevent algae bloom.

Craigencalt Farm lies above with the popular Barn at the Loch eatery and farm shop (open all year). Tucked in here too is Earthship Fife, a self-contained eco-house (largely made of car tyres) sunk into the hillside and functioning by a mix of wind, solar and water power. There's also a yurt.

We leave Craigencalt and the loch by the entrance road but soon turn off, right, to reach the Ecology Centre, with its lochside setting. This offers a range of educational and training programmes. Many trees have been planted and there's a training market garden. One group of older men work to refurbish garden and other tools which are then sent off to projects in Africa.

From the loch's outflow a path leads to the B923 again. Walk left till safe to cross and head down the Burnside Path (signed). Take care crossing! There's a big housing development up left. A small reservoir is passed (bulrushes). Reaching the first houses of Kinghorn go up, right, to come on the fine Kinghorn Golf Course and walk down its edge to a gate at the back of the Primary School. Turn along and then right which brings you to the centre of Kinghorn.

The building on the corner (facing the war memorial) was the offices of Gibson's, the first golf club manufacturer in Scotland. At its peak 100 dozen hand-forged heads a week were being turned out. Cross to the war memorial, the work of Alexander Carrick (who also did the figure of Wallace at the entrance to Edinburgh Castle). One name was added for the grim Korean War and there's a special mention of Sgt. John McAulay, born in Kinghorn, and already awarded a DCM, who then, in November 1917, won a VC for unimaginable heroics. Happy to relate, he survived three years of horror to return to his police profession, and reach the rank of Inspector. He died in 1956.

Head off down Rossland Place. On the right is the old primary school, now a community centre with sports facilities, a café and the Community Library. Cross over to the white building (top of Harbour Road) and, to its right, into the carpark of Harbour View (restaurant etc.) from whence head seawards to rejoin the FCP on the Quarrel Braes.

Appendix 2
Largo Law

Largo Law, at 290m. (952ft.) may not be a big hill, but its isolated stance above the Forth makes it a grandstand viewpoint and a climb is recommended, either as part of the coastal walk or at another time. The only recognised route is from the primary school on a minor road leading inland from Upper Largo, itself with some historical interests. Oddly, there is no prehistoric fort on the summit.

If aiming for Largo Law from Lower Largo, turn up the small tarred road nearing the end of the town to gain the historic Serpentine Walk. This wends up a den (dell) under the care of the Woodland Trust to reach the A915 coastal road, which is followed up into Upper Largo. The road swings sharp right at the hotel. On the left is the minor road we follow.

Upper Largo is also Kirkton of Largo and the church, off left, has a Pictish stone at the entrance with a hunting scene

Largo Law, rising from the rich Fife farmland.

Upper Largo's historic church and Largo Law.

and one of the mysterious 'swimming beasts'. A gravestone at the right side of the church has El Greco-like elongated figures and a sad story to tell. Continue up the country road (North Feus). Across the road nearing the primary school is a pillared gateway (not used). Looking down from there a hollow is seen curving across a field towards a pepperpot tower. This is the course of the first-ever canal cut in Scotland, in the fifteenth century, for Sir Andrew Wood, local chiel and naval hero, who was rowed to church in his admiral's barge by captured English sailors. Wood was a successful merchant who had proved his capabilities against pirates and enemy attacks, so James III made him admiral. He also served the brilliant James IV. Early in the latter's reign, though not at war, five armed English merchantmen attacked shipping in the Forth. Wood, with just two ships, captured all five. Henry VIII was not amused and sent Stephen Bull with three ships of war to capture or destroy Wood. Wood, returning from Flanders with the *Yellow Carvel* and *Flower*, was attacked off the May and the battle raged all day and night, ending off Fife Ness with Bull's surrender. The crews were repatriated—after the lower deck prisoners dug his canal. Wood oversaw the construction of the *Great Michael* (much bigger than the *Mary Rose*) whose building devastated Fife's woods. The pepperpot tower (doocot at one state) is all that remains of the castle he built. He is buried in the church.

Another (John) Wood (a descendant), who died in 1681, had been a royalist courtier and left quite a fortune for a *hospital* (hospice) for 'indigent and enfeebled men'—who had to bear the name Wood. Rebuilt in the 1830s in Jacobean mansion style, the building still offers sheltered housing for the elderly, but no longer all having to have the same surname.

Between school and cemetery is a car park from where the Largo Law walk begins. The route edges a field, passes a row of neatly restored cottages and goes on to Chesterstone Farm. Skirt the farm, left, to turn sharp left, uphill, on a green track aiming straight at Largo Law. Rough pasture with gorse leads steeply up the final cone above the arable level. Cows may be grazing, so observe the country code. There's a false top, then a dip (with a stile over a fence), to reach the 290m. trig point, the highest point along the Fife coast. The ascent is unrelentingly steep (it is a volcanic cone) but is rewarded by a huge view of the outer Forth estuary, just as the Binn gave the inner Forthj view. The view north takes in a horizon of Highland hills behind Sidlaws, Ochils and Lomonds. (I once spotted the Law from Lochnagar.) The summit has yellow violets, bedstraw, buttercups and cuckoo flowers. Retrace the upward route exactly back to the primary school.

If the start was made at Lower Largo a good circular walk is possible rather than just backtracking. Turn right on joining the wee road past the school, and opposite the upper cemetery gates go left along a field edge path. There's a glimpse of Andrew Wood's tower, the sad ruin of Largo Home Farm and a lectern-type doocot for the 1750 John Adam mansion, itself now gone. A small road is crossed (caravan park on the right) and the continuation leads to Keil's Den, another Woodland Trust dell. This is followed down, then left, to exit to the minor road crossed earlier. Turn down to cross the A915 back to Lower Largo.

Appendix 3
The Chain Walk

I first came on the Chain Walk as a youth, more years ago than I'll admit, and was fascinated by it and have done it many times since. Being curious about when it was made I had visions of Victorian ladies in their long skirts swinging along the chains. The date was clarified when I met an old lady who said, as a young girl, she had helped to drag chains along to the site—in 1929. Britain's first *via ferrata*. Eventually it became rather decayed, the rock weathered, chains were missing or dangerously rusty, so Fife Council repaired some of the worst spots only to be told they had thereby taken on responsibility for the site. So they replaced the lot. And sometime later, thieves stole all the chains! Replacing them again, as we see today, cost £30,000.

The Chain Walk is more often done from the Earlsferry end, but this description is given as better suiting FCP walkers. Doing it, walkers become climbers. It is not for the fainthearted. A word of warning, the Chain Walk is a potentially dangerous

Steps and chains for one descent on the 'walk'.

Working along the Chain Walk.

undertaking, involving dangling across cliffs on chains, sometimes above the sea, with strenuous ascents and descents. It
is not practical at high tide, and a start should only be made
from half ebb to half flow. An hour at least is needed by the
competent to complete the route. In many places bucket
steps have been cut, but weathering has made some of these
precarious, and the rock is greasy when wet. There are no
escape routes. Treat the fun passage seriously; it is a unique
entertainment. You tackle it at your own risk!

On descending the initial slope to rock level you'll see a
rectangular cave set in the back of a cove to the right: the Devil's Cave, which runs in a surprising distance. The approach
is by a shallow gully seawards, so only practical at low tide.
The Chain Walk is round to the left from the zigzag descent.
Don't drop too far down as easier ground tempts, but keep a
higher traverse which leads to the first short chain down into
a cove (one shallow, one deeper cave), then a traverse of cliff
with horizontal chains for security. This leads to a vertical
chain in a corner, the longest haul upwards, but eased by cut
steps once above the overhanging start. There's an iron post
on the neck at the top.

Beyond is a beach with a huge inter-tide flat area marked
with lines of dykes so straight they look man-made. There
are pinnacles and spikes worn out of the breccias of the point
and the sea surges in deep-cut gullies. The flat area ends at

Kincraig Point itself. A wall of organ-pipes (columnar basalt) will entertain, then there is another vertical chain to haul up, then we head down the other side into a wee bay where we swing left to a marked neck in another lava-flow. A short chain leads down to the major area of geological interest. There's a big spread of soaring basalt pillars above a 'scree' of disintegrated hexagonal pieces. A huge grouping of pillars is detached and leans precariously against the main wall. Beyond, the sea-sculpted stumps of long-gone pillars have weathered into what looks a bit like a limestone pavement. The grey shingle has been tumbled into appealing smoothness, often nesting in sea-hollows in the rocks.

From the far top end of the shingle, steps lead up to traverse along the rocks and round a point. Large steps lead down to one of those strange flat areas. Head up left of a natural arch. (Except at low tide it does not offer a way through.) The cliffs are at their most impressive above, beetling out in big belly-folds of rock, noisy with fulmars in the first half of the year.

The next (last) cove is the most serious. Look across at the far side: horizontal chains (with steps cut) lead out to a ledge and down to a lower one—which, at low tide, can be reached from the beach by big steps. The innermost chain can be avoided too but, at high tide, the water will be over the steps in the rock. The way down into the cove is the crux of the whole venture, and can be rather intimidating. One traverses down and along, to then step across a gap onto a detached fin of rock in the cove itself. There are excellent handholds and technically it is not difficult with care. Lean well out so you can spot the holds; cringing in simply constricts and blinds. Avoid the back of the cove (where there are fallen rocks) and go along the horizontal chains as much as the tide dictates or the spirit moves. When the chain ends the route is *down*, on steps almost weathered away, easiest taken facing in. The lower ledge can be slippery. And that is it! Easy going leads down to the warm-coloured sands of Earlsferry.

Appendix 4
May Island

The May is a renowned National Nature Reserve with a residential observatory. A warden will meet visiting boats, while there is plenty of information in the Visitor Centre (toilets). There are daily sailings in the summer months, weather permitting, and times may vary depending on the state of the tide. Usually three hours ashore is given. If a visit is taken in during walking the coast, it is satisfying to know the Isle of May lies 56km./35 miles east of the Forth Bridge. The island is a tilted slab of basalt with stark, dark cliffs, which are a bedlam of birds in season. Sailings usually circle the island when seals can be observed as well.

David I (the deeply religious king) gave the island to the Berkshire Benedictine monastery of Reading, but it had a stormy history of pillage and natural harshness, and when it was transferred to the see of St Andrews following the Battle of Bannockburn (1314) the monks transferred to Pittenweem and the island's ecclesiastical importance disappeared. Only recently have archaeologists been investigating these years of occupancy, well described on-site. The Northern Lighthouse Board purchased the May in 1815 and Robert Stevenson built the present handsome light in the centre of the island in 1816. Sir Walter Scott successfully pleaded for the old light not to be destroyed.

Next to it are the lower parts of the seventeenth-century light. Once higher, it had a grate on top where a fire beacon consumed a ton of coal per night and needed constant attention. Shipping had to pay for this service, the first of its kind anywhere in Scotland. The cinders piled up round the building with tragic results, for, with no light showing on one occasion, investigation found the keeper, his wife and five children all dead in their beds from carbon monoxide poisoning. The very first keeper drowned in a storm, and a poor Anstruther woman was accused of causing this and strangled and burnt as a witch.

The Low Light dates to 1843, and, with the main light, allowed a fix on the treacherous Carr Rocks off Fife Ness. Despite the lights, the nineteenth century saw 39 ships wrecked on the May. The Latvian *Mars* (wrecked in North Ness on what

Old and New Lights on the May.

are now Mars Rocks) and the Danish *Island* (at Colmshole) are still visible hulks. The latter was once the Danish royal yacht. Two Royal Navy frigates, *Nymphon* and *Pallas*, were wrecked near Dunbar in 1810 because they took limekiln flarings on the Lothian shore for the May's beacon.

On disasters, there was one in 1918 which was covered up at the time, being an unimaginable fiasco, which came to be called 'The Battle of May Island'. Two submarines were sunk, other subs and several surface ships were all severely damaged and over a hundred men lost their lives. A display board across the road from the Fisheries Museum outlines what happened and there's a detailed account in Allan's *The Isle of May*. The story reads like a black comedy. A large naval force (two flotillas) of warships, destroyers and K-boats (the Royal Navy's largest class of submarine) were nearing the May at night, without lights and under radio silence, when minesweepers were spotted ahead. Evasive action resulted in multiple collisions among the K-boats, and warships, which crashed into the submarines or each other.

A year later, the end of World War I saw a happier, un-repeatable spectacle from the May, the sailing past of the surrendered German Grand Fleet: 5 battle cruisers, 9 battle-ships, 7 light cruisers and 49 destroyers, along with all the Royal Navy guardian escorts.

The spectacle I would most like to have seen from the May was the 1995 passing of over one hundred tall ships under sail, heading for Bergen in Norway. During World War II one C. O. stationed on the May was a climber and used to scale the cliffs to collect herring gull eggs which were packed off to a London hospital to supplement the patients' meagre rations—one egg a week I seem to recall (but we kept hens).

Many visitors are particularly interested in birds, and a reg-ular programme of ringing and other studies is maintained. The main observatory was established in 1934. The May is often the first spring or autumn landfall for migrants. Well over 200 species have been recorded. A kittiwake ringed on the May was recovered in Newfoundland, a robin in Spain; conversely, finds include a sparrowhawk ringed in Iceland and a goldcrest ringed in Finland, less than a month before.

There is a great web of marked paths, on which visitors are asked to remain, as it is very easy to disturb nest sites, step on them or collapse burrows. The eagle-eyed may spot sitting eider; they sit tight even when at one's feet. The semi-detached north end, Rona, is kept for research only, no visitors. The Altarstanes at that end is an alternative landing spot, mostly used by divers (human ones, for whom the May is as favoured a spot as it is for ornithologists). The lighthouse has a sprawl of solar panels behind it and there are old, effective, Heligo-land traps for capturing birds. The south end has the most spectacular cliffs, lying beyond the excavated religious ruins. One can reach the south horn; it and the north horn on Rona are long non-operational and the pipes one sees along the way once carried the compressed air to operate them. Guillemots, razorbills, shags, fulmars, kittiwakes and gulls make the cliffs lively (and noisy) and terns have been on the increase, nesting between the landing at Kirkhaven and up round the Visitor Centre, the area most traversed by people. As they dive-bomb people this seems a strange choice and it is now thought the reason is that the humans keep away the gulls which predate their chicks. They use us as a human shield—and still dive at us. The many thousands of puffins are the greatest lure of course and one can see them remarkably close, in season flying

Puffins on the Isle of May.

in with beakfuls of food for their chicks, safe in their burrows. The Bishop is my favourite spot for puffin-watching. They are a great delight. Many years ago I took a school gang to the May. On the way back I noticed the donkey jacket sleeve of one boy was bulging—and moving. A somewhat bedraggled puffin was shaken out and flew off home, hell for feather.

Do visit the excavated site of the early religious settlement, not far from the Visitors' Centre. The *May Princess* carries a maximum 100 passengers, so there is no feeling of being crowded on the island. In summer the slopes can be snowy white with sea campion, thrift nods from the colourful li-chened rocks, the sea shimmers and there are vast skyscapes.

Acknowledgements

I'd like to thank several people for researching on my behalf: Richard Cormack, Steve Hindley, Simon and Hilary Payne, Adrian Snowball; and Roger Diggins for more practical help. There were many people met along the way over the years whose names were never known and, in 2020, when public transport alone was possible, I owe a great deal to the drivers of Fife buses and trains for the many complex journeys I had to make—and to Jim, of Aly's Taxi Service in Cupar, for taking me to and fro to access the northern hills.

I'm indebted to two friends in the St Andrews Photographic Society for striking images: Richard Cormack for the Queensferry Crossing bridge and Jan-Karel Querido for the St Monans zig-zag breakwater, and to George and Kath McQuitty for the author shot and the Wormit VR post box, and to the McKenzie Smith family for the Lindores Distillery image. My photographic archive is held in the University of St Andrews Library Special Collections and I'm grateful to Rachel Nordstrom and Jane Campbell for access and for seeing the new slides required were scanned and made available. From the older book I'd like to thank again those who allowed me to take on-site, indoor photographs: Burntisland Parish Church for the gallery ship on fire picture; the Scottish Fisheries Museum for the model expert at work; Historic Scotland for the figure of John Knox preaching, in St Andrews Castle; and the British Golf Museum, St Andrews, for the old-time figure making a golf ball by hand.

There wouldn't be a book but for the Fife Coast and Countryside Trust and their creation of the Fife Coastal Path, an ongoing work of maintenance and improvement. Following the difficult time of 2020, may the team continue their good work which walkers appreciate.

I'd like to thank Helen Stirling for drawing the new maps for this edition, Roger Smith for proofing and indexing it, and Hugh Andrew and Andrew Simmons at Birlinn for their support while it was being prepared. The main task of turning my material into a book fell to Tom Johnstone, work completed during the difficult months of the coronavirus outbreak. A very big thank you.

Index